THE

INSTANT

COIN

COLLECTOR

2ND EDITION

Everything You Need to Know
to Get Started Now

ARLYN G. SIEBER

Published by

Krause Publications, a division of F+W Media, Inc.
700 East State Street • Iola, WI 54990-0001
715-445-2214 • 888-457-2873
www.krausebooks.com

To order books or other products call toll-free 1-800-258-0929
or visit us online at www.shopnumismaster.com

ISBN-13: 978-1-4402-3707-2
ISBN-10: 1-4402-3707-7

Designed by Jana Tappa
Edited by Caitlin Spaulding

Printed in China

ACKNOWLEDGMENTS

The author gratefully acknowledges the following for their assistance in producing this book:

Heritage Auctions
Kris Kandler
Chet Krause
U.S. Mint
Chris Williams

And previous Krause Publications authors whose work provided the basic knowledge for the text that follows.

CONTENTS

PART 3: WHAT TO WATCH FOR

PART 4: SPEAKING OF COINS

PART 5: TAKING THE NEXT STEP

PART 1

GETTING A HANDLE ON COINS

Basic tips for starting out right

WELCOME TO COIN COLLECTING

A GOLD STATER OF KING CROESUS OF LYDIA

The kingdom of Lydia, which was located in part of modern-day Turkey, is credited with producing the world's first coins in 700-650 B.C. Some speculate that the world's first coin collector came shortly thereafter.

Coin collecting has provided an enjoyable, educational, and sometimes profitable pastime for generations. The hobby welcomes those of all ages, physical abilities, and financial means. All it requires is an interest in the subject, enjoyment in pursuing a collecting goal, and satisfaction in the completion of that goal. The reward is the pride a collector feels when he or she pulls a coin album off their bookshelf and views a complete collection of a particular coin type or series, or even the progress made toward completing a collection.

Printed references to coin collecting date back as far as the 15th century. In 1796, the hobby generated the first widely circulated book on numismatics: *The Virtuoso's Companion and Coin Collector's Guide*, published in England. Coinage was scarce in Colonial America, so there were few coins to collect and even fewer with the financial wherewithal to put coins aside and not spend them.

1792 HALF DISME

Congress passed an act establishing the U.S. Mint on April 2, 1792. The decimal coinage system it authorized was based largely on a plan put forth by Thomas Jefferson. The following July, it produced 1,500 silver "half dismes," or 5-cent pieces, which are regarded as the nation's first official coinage.

U.S. coinage began in earnest in 1793 with the production of more than 35,000 copper half cents and more than 36,000 copper one-cent coins. By 1796, in addition to half cents and cents, the Mint was producing silver half dimes, dimes, quarters, half dollars, and dollars, and gold $2.50, $5, and $10 coins. By the mid-1800s, the Mint was producing about 17 million coins annually in 12 denominations.

1793 HALF CENT

The increased production meant more coins to collect, and there were more people who could afford to collect them. A few magazines devoted to coin collecting began to appear in the middle of the century. So did dealers who bought and sold collectible coins for a living or as a supplement to their day jobs. The magazines contained advertisements for collectible coins and oftentimes were produced as house organs and marketing tools by the dealers themselves.

Many collectors of the time also courted relationships with banks, bullion exchange houses, or other volume handlers of coins as sources for their collections. Those who lived

1793 ONE CENT

near Philadelphia cultivated relationships with officials and employees of the U.S. Mint's production facility located there and thus obtained coins directly from the mint.

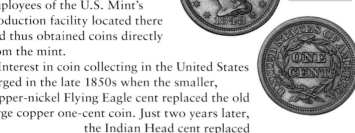

1848 ONE CENT

Interest in coin collecting in the United States surged in the late 1850s when the smaller, copper-nickel Flying Eagle cent replaced the old large copper one-cent coin. Just two years later, the Indian Head cent replaced the Flying Eagle cent. The general public started putting aside the obsolete coins, and demand and prices for them rose. Professional coin dealers emerged to meet the demand, and by the 1870s, most major Eastern cities had coin clubs.

1858 ONE CENT

The next major development in coin collecting occurred in 1888 when Dr. George Heath of Monroe, Michigan – a physician by trade who moonlighted as a mail-order coin dealer – published the first issue of *The American Numismatist*. Like many other publications of the time, the magazine was a marketing tool for Heath's coin business. In his new magazine, the country doctor estimated the number of U.S. coin collectors at 20,000.

By 1891, Heath had shortened the serial's title to *The Numismatist*, and its readership formed the basis for the founding of the American Numismatic Association. The ANA continues today as the nation's largest organization for coin collectors, and *The Numismatist* continues as its official monthly journal.

Coin collecting continued to grow in the early 20th century as exciting new designs made old coins obsolete. Ironically, the Great Depression brought another major development in coin collecting that defined the hobby for years to come and still impacts it today.

In 1934, the Whitman Publishing Company of Racine,

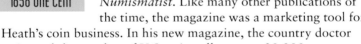

NUMISMATICS (NEW-MISS-MAT-IKS)
The study or collection of coins, tokens, and paper money.

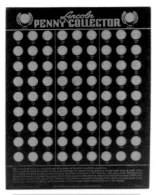

WHITMAN PENNY BOARD

Wisconsin, introduced the "penny board." It was essentially a big piece of cardboard with holes in it for each date and mint mark of Lincoln cents, starting in 1909. The boards sold for 25 cents each and were widely available in hardware stores, dime stores, shoeshine parlors, and gasoline stations.

The boards provided cheap entertainment during the economic struggles of the 1930s as people of all ages checked the one-cent coins in their pocket change for dates and mint marks that would fill an empty hole in the board. In 1940, the board was reconfigured into a blue folder. The blue Whitman folders and similar products from other companies, such as the Warman's line of coin folders, continue today to provide direction in collecting a particular series and a storage and display medium for collectors.

Coin collecting enjoyed a boom period in the 1950s. War veterans and others had disposable income to devote to a hobby and could find coins of the late 1800s and early

U.S. MINT

The official United States Mint (www.usmint.gov) is a branch of the Treasury Department charged with producing the nation's coinage. Its director is appointed by the president.

Private businesses that sometimes concoct official-sounding names that include the words "mint" or "Washington" or other terms sometimes associated with the federal government should not be confused with the official U.S. government mint.

The U.S. Mint's main production facility is located in Philadelphia. Production facilities in Denver, San Francisco, and West Point, New York, are known as branch mints. The U.S. Mint is also in charge of the nation's $100 billion gold and silver reserves. This includes the gold reserves held at the Fort Knox Bullion Depository in Kentucky.

1900s in circulation. What they couldn't find, they could buy from the growing number of dealers who operated shops, set up at coin shows, or advertised in coin publications such as the newly founded *Numismatic News*.

AMERICAN NUMISMATIC ASSOCIATION

818 North Cascade Avenue
Colorado Springs, CO 80903
(719) 632-2646
www.money.org

Today, coin collecting is enjoying another renaissance thanks in part to U.S. Mint programs such as the America the Beautiful Quarters and other collectible series. Many cities and even smaller towns have coin shops. Major coin auction houses make national headlines when they sell some of numismatics' great rarities. Local, state, and regional organizations for coin collectors meet regularly and sponsor shows where collectors can browse the offerings of dozens or even hundreds of dealers in one spot. Many of these shows also feature non-commercial displays of coins and other numismatic items set up by collectors to the benefit of their fellow hobbyists.

The ANA sponsors two shows annually in different cities across the nation. In addition to the bourse floor, the gatherings offer seminars and organization meetings that promote education and camaraderie among fellow collectors. The ANA's headquarters in Colorado Springs, Colorado, features a world-class museum open to all and an extensive reference library that members can use for free.

The purpose of this book is to help prospective coin collectors get off to a good start that can lead to a lifetime of enjoyment. Part 1 covers some of the basics one needs to know before popping that first coin in an album.

Part 2 covers various series of coins that new collectors can consider for their first pursuit. The emphasis is on coins that can be collected from circulation or purchased at low cost. Some lament that "valuable" coins, such as those collectors were plucking from circulation in the 1950s, can't be found in

BOURSE (BORS)

The area of a coin show or convention where dealers offer coins for sale. It is often set up in a hotel ballroom or main hall of a convention center.

COIN SHOWS BIG AND SMALL BRING TOGETHER COLLECTORS AND DEALERS

circulation anymore. But many of the coins that today's veteran hobbyists cut their collecting teeth on weren't "valuable" at the time and have never become valuable. The emphasis wasn't on value; it was on the satisfaction and enjoyment of building a collection. It was on the thrill of finding a long-sought piece needed for a collection.

Having said that, there are still "valuable" coins that can be found in circulation. They may be scarce, but the odds of actually finding one or more increase when collectors know what's valuable and what to look for. Part 3 covers various series or varieties to watch for when searching circulating coins.

Part 4 provides an illustrated guide to coin terms and an introduction to the all-important topic of grading coins. Part 5 provides tips on taking the next step once a collector feels he or she has mastered the basics. It includes information on the coin community – organizations, publications, and Web sites – and comments and tips on collecting more expensive coins.

ANA MUSEUM

Welcome to coin collecting. It is a pursuit rich in tradition and history, but it is also a field with exciting new issues and opportunities for the future.

CHAPTER 1

HOW TO HANDLE AND STORE COINS

So you're about to get a bunch of coins. Now what?

A pile of coins in a coffee can or a shoebox or wrapped up in rolls is just a pile of coins. But organizing them so they can be conveniently stored in some orderly system and viewed on demand makes them a collection. It also preserves them for the long term. They're no longer subject to the wear and tear of circulation.

Many of the suggested series for new collectors covered in Part 2 of this book can be found in circulation or purchased at low cost. Handling and storage considerations for these low-cost coins aren't as critical as they are for, say, a rare silver dollar worth thousands. Still, good habits formed early in a collecting life will pay off later when a collector moves up in rarity and price.

HOW TO HANDLE COINS

The less coins are handled, the better. Dirty, oily hands – even if they appear to be clean – lead to dirty, oily coins.

Oftentimes, however, coins have to be handled, particularly when searching circulating coins or when transferring a coin to a holder. When it is necessary to handle a coin, it should be held by the edges between the thumb and forefinger. Avoid contact with the coin's obverse and reverse surfaces.

Also, handle coins over a soft surface so they will not be damaged if accidentally dropped.

SHOULD I CLEAN MY COINS?

No.

Luster is an important aspect when grading certain high-end coins, but in general, a coin's grade and its corresponding value depend on the amount of wear on the coin, not how shiny it is. Cleaning – particularly home-brewed methods – is often abrasive and will damage a coin rather than improve it.

There may be certain instances when it is desirable to clean a coin, but that is best left to experienced opinions as to when and how.

HOW TO STORE COINS

▶ FOLDERS

Cardboard folders are the most inexpensive and common form of organizing and storing a collection. They can be purchased at many hobby shops and bookstores. The Warman's line of coin folders can be purchased online at www.shopnumismaster.com.

They provide a spot for each date and mintmark in a particular series, thus acting as a road map for the collector. They are also compact and convenient; they take up little space on a bookshelf and can be pulled down and opened for easy viewing.

The spots for the coins consist of holes in the cardboard sized specially for the particular series covered by the folder. They are meant to be a tight fit so the coins, once inserted, won't fall out.

FOLDERS

Place the coin in the hole at an angle, so one side of the coin is in the hole. On the side of the coin sticking up, press down and toward the angled side until the coin snaps into place.

The process isn't always graceful; thus, some of the basic rules for handling coins have to be suspended when working with folders. But folders are still suitable for storing coins plucked from circulation and getting started in coin collecting.

▶ 2-BY-2S

Low to moderately priced coins offered for sale at shops and shows are usually stored in cardboard holders commonly called "2-by-2s" because they are 2 inches square. They consist of two

2-BY-2S

pieces with a clear Mylar window in the center. The coin is placed between the two pieces, which are then stapled together.

These 2-by-2 holders are also inexpensive. They are suitable for long-term storage and offer a number of advantages over the basic folder:
- The window in the holder allows both sides of the coin to be viewed.
- The entire coin is enclosed.
- The coin can be handled by the edges when being inserted into the holder.

As for disadvantages:
- Storing an entire collection of a particular series takes up more space.
- The coins can be viewed only one at a time.
- Caution should be used when inserting or removing coins from the holders to make sure the staples' sharp edges don't damage the coins.
- There is no road map to the series. A separate checklist is needed.

The 2-by-2 holders can be stored in long, narrow boxes specially sized to hold them. They can also be inserted into pockets in a plastic page, which can then be inserted into a three-ring binder.

Originally the plastic pages contained polyvinylchloride, which produced a soft, flexible pocket. But the substance breaks down over time, resulting in a green slime that could contact the coins. Manufacturers then started substituting Mylar for the PVC. The Mylar does not break down, but the page containing it is more brittle and not as flexible.

▶ FLIPS

Similar in size to the cardboard 2-by-2s, plastic "flips," to use the vernacular, are another common storage method for coins for sale. They consist of a plastic pocket, into which the coin is inserted, with a flap that folds down over the pocket. Coin dealers will often staple the flap shut.

FLIPS

Flips offer many of the same advantages as the cardboard 2-by-2s:

– Although they cost more, flips are still inexpensive.
– The entire coin is enclosed.
– Both sides of the coin can be viewed.
– The coin can be handled by the edges when being inserted into the holder.

Also, they don't have to be stapled shut, thus eliminating the possibility of the staples scratching the coin.

The big disadvantage to flips is their composition. They, too, originally contained polyvinylchloride. Manufacturers then started making flips containing Mylar, but the resulting product again is more brittle and not as flexible as the old PVC flips.

For long-term storage, it's best to remove coins from flips and transfer them to another type of holder.

▶ ALBUMS

Coin albums are a step up from the basic folder. They are in book form and contain a hole for each date and mintmark in the particular series covered. The hole has a clear plastic back and a clear plastic front. The plastic front slides out, and the coin can be placed in the hole. The plastic front is then slid back over the hole.

Albums combine many of the advantages of 2-by-2s and folders:

– They are compact and convenient, and can be stored on a bookshelf.
– They are affordable.
– Both sides of the coin can be viewed.

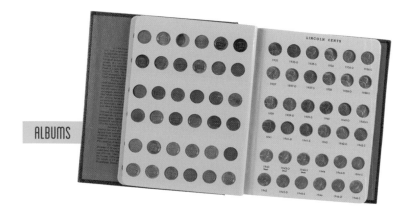

ALBUMS

– Their labeled holes act as a road map to a series.

– The entire coin is enclosed.

– The coin can be handled by the edges when being inserted.

The disadvantage to albums is that sliding the plastic front can damage a coin in the holder if the plastic rubs against the coin. Thus, albums are not recommended for expensive uncirculated coins.

▶ HARD-PLASTIC HOLDERS

Hard-plastic holders are the top of the line in coin shortage but are still affordable. They consist of two pieces with one or more clear windows through which the coin can be viewed. The two pieces are held together with plastic screws or snap together.

HARD-PLASTIC HOLDERS

To insert a coin into the holder, the two pieces are separated and the coin is placed face up into the bottom piece. The top piece is then placed over the bottom piece, and the two pieces are screwed or snapped together again.

Some of the world's great numismatic rarities are stored in hard-plastic holders. They offer all of the advantages of the less expensive storage methods but in a safe, inert environment.

GRADED COINS IN SLABS

► SLABS

In 1986, a group of coin dealers got together and formed the Professional Coin Grading Service. For a fee, dealers and collectors could submit coins to the service and receive a professional opinion on their grades. After grading, a coin is encapsulated in an inert hard-plastic holder with a serial number and the service's opinion on its grade indicated on the holder.

The concept was successful, and several competing services were established in succeeding years. Today, most coins valuable enough to justify the grading fee have been graded by one of the services and encapsulated in its holder.

The grading-service holders are common at coin shows and shops, and acquired the nickname "slabs." The holders are suitable for long-term storage of high-end collectible coins.

TERMS

OBVERSE
The face, or "heads" side, of a coin.

REVERSE
The back, or "tails" side, of a coin.

MINTMARK
A small letter or other mark on a coin indicating where it was minted. Current U.S. coinage carries either a "D" mintmark for Denver, "P" for Philadelphia, "S" for San Francisco, or "W" for West Point, New York. U.S. coins without mintmarks were minted at Philadelphia.

MYLAR
A DuPont trademark for a strong polyester film.

PART 2

HOW TO GET STARTED

Coin series and strategies
for new collectors

CHAPTER 2

COLLECTING LINCOLN MEMORIAL CENTS

sk a longtime coin collector about the first series he or she collected, and they will probably say Lincoln cents. U.S. 1-cent coins have been a staple for new collectors since the Whitman Publishing Company introduced its venerable "penny board" in the 1930s. This tradition continued as the board morphed into a folder in the 1940s.

The U.S. Mint now produces billions of 1-cent coins a year, so there is little to no chance that any one of them popped into a folder today will command a substantial numismatic premium in the future. But the basic premise of collecting 1-cent coins – the satisfaction of pursuing and ultimately completing a series collection – has not changed since the penny board was introduced in 1934.

The collecting knowledge gained by pursuing 1-cent coins can provide the foundation for a positive experience when moving up the collecting value ladder. Any mistakes made at this level are a cheap education that can pay off big time in the future.

THE STORY BEHIND THE COIN

The Lincoln cent was introduced in 1909 to commemorate the centennial of Abraham Lincoln's birth. Lincoln thus became the first president to be depicted on circulating U.S. coinage.

Designer Victor David Brenner fashioned the bust of Lincoln on the obverse. His design for the reverse consisted of the words "One Cent" framed by two wheat ears. Lincoln cents with this reverse design are commonly referred to as "wheat cents."

The reverse design was changed in 1959 to commemorate the 150th anniversary of Lincoln's birth. Designer Frank Gasparro composed a depiction of the Lincoln Memorial in Washington, D.C., which replaced the wheat-ears design on the reverse. The Lincoln Memorial reverse was used through 2008.

1932-D LINCOLN CENT

LINCOLN MEMORIAL CENT SPECS

Obverse designer: Victor David Brenner.

Reverse designer: Frank Gasparro.

Diameter: 19 millimeters.

Composition (1959-1982): copper-zinc.

Weight (1959-1982): 3.11 grams.

Composition (1982-2008): copper-plated zinc.

Weight (1982-2008): 2.5 grams.

WHERE TO GET THEM

Sources for a Lincoln Memorial cent collection are as close as one's pocket.

Collectors can check their pocket change for dates and mintmarks that fill empty spots in their collection.

Pocket change is a particularly good source for recent-year issues. Clean, brightly colored specimens with little wear can be found and put aside for a collection. Even older Lincoln Memorial cents, dating back to the 1960s or even 1959, can be found in pocket change.

To fill a collection more quickly, search a larger quantity of coins, such as change from a small business, if possible. Or, obtain several rolls of 1-cent coins from your bank.

In an exercise for this book, five rolls of 1-cent coins (250 coins total) were obtained from a local bank. Also gathered for the exercise was a Warman's folder for Lincoln Memorial cents, a 5X magnifying glass, a container in which the unneeded coins could be placed, and a soft surface on which to work.

LINCOLN-CENT ROLL SEARCH

The search of the five rolls produced 65 of the 105 coins needed to fill the folder's 1959-2008 slots. Predictably, most of the missing coins were the earlier issues, from the 1960s. But the oldest coins found were a 1959-D, 1960-D, and a 1961.

The search took a couple of hours, which can help pass the time on a rainy or snowy weekend afternoon. It can also bring together a parent and child when the search is a joint project between the two.

MINTMARKS

Lincoln Memorial cents struck for circulation have either no mintmark or a "D" indicating the coin was struck at the Denver Mint. Those without mintmarks were struck at either Philadelphia (1959-2008) or West Point (1973-1986).

The San Francisco Mint ("S" mint mark) produced cents for circulation from 1968 through 1974. Starting in 1975, it produced S-mintmark cents for inclusion only in special collector sets (proof and uncirculated sets).

The mintmark appears below the date on the obverse of Lincoln Memorial cents. A magnifying glass helps decipher them.

CENT QUIZ

Question: How many pennies does the U.S. Mint produce in a year?

Answer: None.

Officially, the Mint does not strike "pennies;" it strikes "1-cent coins." A penny is a traditional British denomination.

Although knowledgeable and longtime collectors may still informally call U.S. 1-cent coins "pennies," the majority refer to them more accurately as "cents."

CONDITION

As the rolls were searched in the exercise noted above, coins that filled a hole in the folder were temporarily placed over the hole rather than immediately inserted into it. When a duplicate of a date and mintmark was found, it was compared to the previous example, and the coin in better condition was kept.

When comparing Lincoln cents, it is tempting to automatically keep the shiniest example of a particular date and mintmark. Original, bright-bronze color on a cent does indeed indicate a coin that has seen little circulation.

But also check for wear on the design's high points. On a cent, these include Lincoln's cheekbone and the detail in his hair. A magnifying glass and incandescent lighting aid in examining a coin's condition.

HOW TO STORE THEM

As indicated above, an inexpensive folder is just fine for storing Lincoln Memorial cents plucked from circulation. The 2-by-2 holders could also be used if desired. Or, a collector could keep a few 2-by-2 holders handy in case he or she comes across a coin that, for whatever reason, they deem worthy of a little extra protection.

LINCOLN MEMORIAL CENT CHECKLIST

_____	1959	_____	1969-S
_____	1959-D	_____	1970
_____	1960	_____	1970-D
_____	1960-D	_____	1970-S
_____	1961	_____	1971
_____	1961-D	_____	1971-D
_____	1962	_____	1971-S
_____	1962-D	_____	1972
_____	1963	_____	1972-D
_____	1963-D	_____	1972-S
_____	1964	_____	1973
_____	1964-D	_____	1973-D
_____	1965	_____	1973-S
_____	1966	_____	1974
_____	1967	_____	1974-D
_____	1968	_____	1974-S
_____	1968-D	_____	1975
_____	1968-S	_____	1975-D
_____	1969	_____	1976
_____	1969-D	_____	1976-D

_____ 1977	_____ 1993
_____ 1977-D	_____ 1993-D
_____ 1978	_____ 1994
_____ 1978-D	_____ 1994-D
_____ 1979	_____ 1995
_____ 1979-D	_____ 1995-D
_____ 1980	_____ 1996
_____ 1980-D	_____ 1996-D
_____ 1981	_____ 1997
_____ 1981-D	_____ 1997-D
_____ 1982	_____ 1998
_____ 1982-D	_____ 1998-D
_____ 1983	_____ 1999
_____ 1983-D	_____ 1999-D
_____ 1984	_____ 2000
_____ 1984-D	_____ 2000-D
_____ 1985	_____ 2001
_____ 1985-D	_____ 2001-D
_____ 1986	_____ 2002
_____ 1986-D	_____ 2002-D
_____ 1987	_____ 2003
_____ 1987-D	_____ 2003-D
_____ 1988	_____ 2004
_____ 1988-D	_____ 2004-D
_____ 1989	_____ 2005
_____ 1989-D	_____ 2005-D
_____ 1990	_____ 2006
_____ 1990-D	_____ 2006-D
_____ 1991	_____ 2007
_____ 1991-D	_____ 2007-D
_____ 1992	_____ 2008
_____ 1992-D	_____ 2008-D

CHANGE IN THE CHANGE

In 1982, the cent's composition changed from predominately copper alloyed with zinc to predominately zinc plated with copper. Coins in both compositions were struck in that year.

They can be distinguished by weight. The predominately copper composition weighs 3.11 grams; the predominately zinc composition weighs 2.5 grams.

Some folders contain holes for both compositions. Collectors without the means to weigh the coins should not fret this distinction in compiling their collections. There is no difference in numismatic value between the two compositions in circulated grades.

GET IN THE LOUPE

A magnifying glass is an essential tool of coin collecting. It allows a collector to view details on a coin, especially when examining a coin's condition.

A glass of about 5X is fine for most beginning to intermediate coin-collecting pursuits and is affordable.

MAGNIFYING GLASS

COIN QUIZ

Question: How many images of Lincoln appear on the Lincoln Memorial cent?

Answer: Two.
The first, of course, is the bust of Lincoln on the obverse. For the second, look closely in the middle of the Lincoln Memorial on the reverse on a newer cent. An outline of the Lincoln statue that appears in the real Lincoln Memorial can be seen on the coin.

SMALL VS. LARGE

There are three years of circulating Lincoln Memorial cents –
1960, 1970, and 1982 – with slight design variations in the dates.
These are commonly referred to as "small date" and "large date"
because of the difference in size between the two variations.

The 1960 small date struck at Philadelphia is worth about
$2 retail in higher circulated grades, but the rest do not vary
substantially above face value in circulated grades.

Some folders or albums may contain holes for the date
variations.

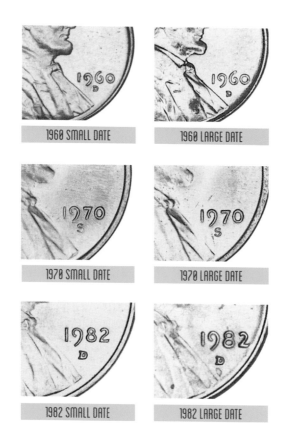

1960 SMALL DATE 1960 LARGE DATE

1970 SMALL DATE 1970 LARGE DATE

1982 SMALL DATE 1982 LARGE DATE

CHAPTER 3

COLLECTING LINCOLN BICENTENNIAL AND UNION SHIELD CENTS

The 2009 Lincoln Bicentennial cents, and their Union Shield successor starting in 2010, give new collectors and others who collect from circulation an excellent opportunity to get in on the ground floor of a new series. Uncirculated and proof examples originally sold by the U.S. Mint are available on the secondary market, but nice examples of newly or recently minted coins are available in circulation too.

THE STORY BEHIND THE COINS

The Lincoln cent was originally introduced in 1909 to commemorate the centennial of Abraham Lincoln's birth. The cent's reverse was changed in 1959, from the original wheat-ears design to a new Lincoln Memorial design, to commemorate the 150th anniversary of Lincoln's birth. So it was fitting to mark the bicentennial of the 16th president's birth in 2009 by again redesigning the cent.

Title III of the Presidential $1 Coin Act of 2005 directed the U.S. Mint to issue four different circulating 1-cent coins in 2009 to commemorate the bicentennial of Lincoln's birth. The law directed that the Victor David Brenner bust of Lincoln continue on the obverses of the new coins. It further directed that four different reverses be released at quarterly intervals during the year. The first reverse was to be emblematic of Lincoln's birth and early childhood in Kentucky; the second, his formative years in Indiana; the third, his professional life in Illinois; and the fourth, his presidency.

Reverse design for the first coin, released January 12, 2009, depicts a log cabin with Lincoln's birth year, 1809, below. The second reverse design, released May 14, 2009, shows a young Lincoln sitting on a log reading a book with an ax at his side. Lincoln loved to read and often took a book with him to read during breaks in his work on his family's southern Indiana farm.

The third reverse, released August 13, 2009, shows Lincoln

standing in front of what is now the Old State Capitol in Springfield, Illinois. Lincoln was elected to the Illinois General Assembly in 1834, earned his law license in 1836, and was elected to the U.S. House of Representatives in 1846. The fourth reverse, released November 12, 2009, shows the U.S. Capitol with its dome half finished. The design symbolizes the nation torn apart by the Civil War during Lincoln's presidency. The current Capitol dome was still under construction when Lincoln was first inaugurated in 1861. It was completed in 1863, and Lincoln's body lay in state under the dome after he died on April 15, 1865.

Lincoln Bicentennial cents struck for circulation contain the predominately zinc composition used for circulating cents since 1982. The law authorizing the bicentennial coins also stipulated that the Mint issue the coins in a predominately copper composition for "numismatic purposes." The copper versions use the same specifications as the original Lincoln cent in 1909 and were struck in proof and uncirculated versions for sale to collectors.

The authorizing law further stipulated that beginning in 2010, the Lincoln-cent reverse design should symbolize Lincoln's preservation of the United States as a single, unified country. The design chosen shows the Union Shield with the inscription "E Pluribus Unum" at the top. Draped across the shield is a scroll with the words "One Cent" on it.

The shield consists of 13 vertical stripes, representing the original 13 states. The bar across the top with the "E Pluribus Unum" inscription ("Out of Many, One") represents the uniting of the states.

2009 LINCOLN BICENTENNIAL CENTS PROOF SET

WHERE TO GET THEM

A close watch on pocket change, possibly supplemented by roll searches, should yield many if not all of the circulating examples of the Lincoln Bicentennial cents and nice examples with the Union Shield reverse. The Union Shield reverse gives collectors a rare opportunity to start and maintain a new series from circulation, just as collectors did in 1959 when the Lincoln Memorial reverse was introduced.

At their time of issue, the 2009 Lincoln Bicentennial cents were also available in uncirculated and proof versions for purchase directly from the Mint in the sets listed below. All proof versions of the Lincoln Bicentennial cents were struck in their traditional 95-percent-copper composition.

(1) As part of the 2009 annual proof set.

(2) As part of the 2009 annual silver proof set, which contains 90-percent-silver versions of the dime, District of Columbia and U.S. Territories Quarters, and half dollar.

(3) As a four-coin proof set containing only the cents.

(4) As part of the 2009 annual uncirculated set with the cents in the traditional 95-percent-copper composition.

(5) As part of the 2009 Lincoln Coin and Chronicles Set. The set contains proof versions of the 2009 Lincoln commemorative silver dollar and proof versions of the 2009 Lincoln Bicentennial cents.

SPECS

LINCOLN BICENTENNIAL AND UNION SHIELD CENT SPECS

Obverse designer: Victor David Brenner.

Reverse designers: Richard Masters (log cabin), Charles Vickers (Lincoln reading), Joel Iskowitz (Old State Capitol), Susan Gamble (U.S. Capitol), and Lyndall Bass (Union Shield).

Diameter: 19 millimeters.

Copper-plated zinc composition (circulation strikes): 97.5-percent zinc, 2.5-percent copper.

Copper composition (proof versions): 95-percent copper, 5-percent tin and zinc.

Weight: 2.5 grams (zinc composition) and 3.11 grams (copper composition).

The set also contains other souvenir items, such as a reproduction of the Gettysburg Address in Lincoln's handwriting.

These sets are no longer available from the Mint but are available on the secondary market – coin shops, coin shows, and advertisements in hobby publications like *Coins* magazine.

MINTMARKS

Lincoln Bicentennial cents struck for circulation have either no mintmark, indicating they were produced at Philadelphia, or a "D" mintmark for the Denver Mint. All proof versions have an "S" mintmark for the San Francisco Mint.

CONDITION

The same guidelines for grading Lincoln Memorial cents, as found in Chapter 2, apply to the Lincoln Bicentennial cents and Union Shield cents.

HOW TO STORE THEM

Folders are fine for storing Lincoln Bicentennial and Union Shield cents plucked from circulation. Uncirculated and proof versions purchased on the secondary market should be stored in 2-by-2 holders or their original Mint packaging.

THE CENT'S FUTURE

Is the day coming when the U.S. Mint will stop producing 1-cent coins? Probably.

The cent's future has been debated for decades now. As prices for goods and services continue to rise, the purchasing power of the cent continues to decline, to the point where it is negligible today.

Also, as metals prices continue to rise, it now costs the Mint more than 1 cent to produce a 1-cent coin. And most purchases today are paid for with credit or debit cards.

A number of other countries have eliminated their 1-cent counterparts. Canada did so in 2013.

A few consumers still count out some 1-cent coins for cash purchases, and collectors, of course, still love the lowly cent. But all indications are that the 1-cent coin eventually will join 2-cent and 3-cent coins as an obsolete denomination.

LINCOLN BICENTENNIAL CENTS CHECKLIST

► LOG CABIN

_____ 2009 zinc

_____ 2009-D zinc

_____ 2009 copper (uncirculated)

_____ 2009-D copper (uncirculated)

_____ 2009-S copper (proof)

► LINCOLN READING

_____ 2009 zinc

_____ 2009-D zinc

_____ 2009 copper (uncirculated)

_____ 2009-D copper (uncirculated)

_____ 2009-S copper (proof)

► OLD ILLINOIS STATE CAPITOL

_____ 2009 zinc

_____ 2009-D zinc

_____ 2009 copper (uncirculated)

_____ 2009-D copper (uncirculated)

_____ 2009-S copper (proof)

► U.S. CAPITOL

_____ 2009 zinc

_____ 2009-D zinc

_____ 2009 copper (uncirculated)

_____ 2009-D copper (uncirculated)

_____ 2009-S copper (proof)

UNION SHIELD CENT CHECKLIST

► CIRCULATION STRIKES

_____ 2010

_____ 2010-D

_____ 2011

_____ 2011-D

_____ 2012

_____ 2012-D

_____ 2013

_____ 2013-D

Series is ongoing.

CHAPTER 4

COLLECTING THE WESTWARD JOURNEY NICKELS SERIES

'OCEAN IN VIEW!' NICKEL REVERSE

The year 2004 saw the first significant change in the design of the Jefferson 5-cent coin since its introduction in 1938. The result is a short series with pleasing designs that is within the reach of any collector. It's an excellent series for new collectors.

SPECS

JEFFERSON NICKEL SPECS

Obverse designer, 2004: Felix Schlag.

Obverse designers, 2005: Joe Fitzgerald and Don Everhart II.

Obverse designers, 2006: Jamie N. Franki and Donna Weaver.

Reverse designer, 2004 peace medal: Norman E. Nemeth.

Reverse designer, 2004 keelboat: Al Maletsky.

Reverse designers, 2005 bison: Jamie N. Franki and Norman E. Nemeth.

Reverse designers, 2005 "Ocean in view!": Joe Fitzgerald and Donna Weaver.

Reverse designers, 2006 Monticello: Felix Schlag and John Mercanti.

Diameter: 21.2 millimeters.

Composition: copper-nickel.

Weight: 5 grams.

THE STORY BEHIND THE COIN

Felix Schlag's renditions of Thomas Jefferson and his Virginia home, Monticello, made their debut on the 5-cent coin in 1938. They replaced the Buffalo nickel, which remains popular with collectors today.

JEFFERSON NICKEL

The Jefferson nickel saw some changes during the war years of 1942-1945. The composition was changed from copper-nickel to copper, silver, and manganese. To mark the change, the mint mark was moved from below the date on the obverse to above the dome on Monticello on the reverse.

BUFFALO NICKEL

In 1946, the Jefferson nickel reverted to its original composition and design. They remained unchanged until 2004, when Congress authorized new designs to commemorate the bicentennial of Lewis & Clark's exploration of the American West following the Louisiana

WAR NICKEL

Purchase. As president, Jefferson authorized the mission to find the "most direct & practicable water communication across this continent for the purpose of commerce."

FATHER OF THE NATION'S COINAGE

Today's decimal monetary system in the United States is based largely on a proposal put forth by Thomas Jefferson in the country's early days. His original coinage plan called for the dollar as the basic monetary unit and included several minor coins and a gold $10.

2004 PEACE-MEDAL NICKEL

THE STORY BEHIND THE DESIGNS

For 2004, the obverse retained Schlag's bust of Jefferson, which was originally based on a bust by sculptor Jean-Antoine Houdon. The two reverses for 2004 are known as the peace-medal design and the keelboat design.

The peace-medal design is based on the original design for an Indian peace medal commissioned for Lewis & Clark's expedition. It features two clasped hands. The wrist of one hand is adorned with the cuff of a military uniform; the wrist of the other hand is adorned with beads and a stylized American eagle.

The design was meant to symbolize friendship between the American government and the Native Americans that Lewis & Clark would encounter on their exploration. Lewis & Clark carried the medals with them and gave them to Native American leaders as a goodwill gesture.

The keelboat design depicts the type of watercraft Lewis & Clark used in their expedition. The two uniformed figures in the boat's bow represent the two explorers.

For 2005, the traditional bust of Jefferson on the obverse was replaced by another design also

2004 KEELBOAT NICKEL REVERSE

OBVERSE AND REVERSE OF 2005 BISON NICKEL

OBVERSE AND REVERSE OF 'OCEAN IN VIEW!' NICKEL

OBVERSE AND REVERSE OF 2011 JEFFERSON NICKEL

based on a Houdon sculpture. But instead of the traditional full view, the coin focuses on Jefferson's face from the front hairline of his right temple forward. The word "Liberty" in script on the obverse is based on Jefferson's own handwriting.

Two different reverse designs were also used in 2005 – the American bison design and the "Ocean in view!" design.

The American bison design is reminiscent of the so-called Buffalo nickel, which was struck from 1913 until the Jefferson nickel replaced it in 1938. Lewis & Clark's journals described the animal, which was important to the Native American culture.

The "Ocean in view!" reverse design was inspired by a November 7, 1805, entry in William Clark's journal: "We are in view of the opening of the Ocian, which Creates great joy." The view of the Pacific Ocean in the design is based on a photograph by Andrew E. Cier of Astoria, Oregon.

For 2006, the obverse design changed again. The new image was based on a Rembrandt Peale portrait of Jefferson in 1800, when Jefferson was 57 years old and just before he became president. The word "Liberty" is again in script based on Jefferson's handwriting.

The 2006 reverse returned to the traditional view of Monticello as it originally appeared on the Jefferson nickel. But contemporary Mint engravers enhanced Schlag's original work, restoring more detail and relief to the design.

The result, according to the Mint, is a "crisper and more detailed" image.

MINTMARKS

Westward Journey 5-cent coins struck for circulation have either a "P" mintmark for Philadelphia or a "D" mintmark for Denver. The mintmark appears on the obverse on all of the coins in the series. It is below the date on the 2004 and 2006 issues. It is below the word "Liberty" on the 2005 issues.

WHERE'S THE S?

The San Francisco Mint no longer strikes coins for circulation, but it still produces specially prepared coins for inclusion in collector sets, such as proof sets. These coins have an "S" mintmark.

WHERE TO GET THEM

Nice examples of the Westward Journey Nickel Series are easily found in circulation. A watchful eye on pocket change over time should complete a series collection.

Searching large quantities of change will again speed up the process. A search of five rolls of nickels (200 coins) obtained from a local bank produced six of the 10 reverse-design, date, and mintmark combinations required to complete the series:

(1) 2004-D peace medal.
(2) 2004-D keelboat.
(3) 2005-D bison.
(4) 2005-D "Ocean in view!"
(5) 2006-P Monticello.
(6) 2006-D Monticello.

It also produced duplicates for each date, which filled the holes for display of the obverse design alongside the reverse designs for each year.

That left just four coins to complete the series:

(1) 2004-P peace medal.
(2) 2004-P keelboat.
(3) 2005-P bison.
(4) 2005-P "Ocean in view!"

The lack of Philadelphia-produced coins in the sample rolls probably reflects the region in which they were obtained. Still, a close watch on pocket change or searching additional rolls should eventually complete the collection.

CHECK ALL THE DATES

The distinctive obverse and reverse designs made the Westward Journey 5-cent coins stand out when the rolls were opened and dumped onto a soft surface for examination. But the date on each coin in the rolls was still checked and produced some additional keepers.

They were one 1939 Jefferson 5-cent, one 1940, one 1946-D, two 1961-D coins, one 1963-D, nine 1964 coins (seven with "D" mintmarks and two with no mintmarks, indicating they were struck at Philadelphia), and one 1966. One of the 1964-D coins was in such good condition that it could easily have been mistaken for a more recent issue at first glance.

Putting aside these coins can form the basis for taking the Jefferson series back to its debut in 1938. Because 5-cent coins do not contain precious metals, they have not been cherry-picked over the years as much as the higher denominations, which contained silver until 1965. There are still realistic chances of finding older issues, such as those cited above, in circulation.

OBVERSE AND REVERSE OF 1939 NICKEL

OBVERSE AND REVERSE OF 1940 NICKEL

OBVERSE AND REVERSE OF 1946 NICKEL

CONDITION

As with the search for Lincoln Memorial cents in Chapter 2, duplicates were compared and the better example was kept. As needed examples were found, they were laid over the holes and not inserted into the albums until the search was complete.

On the traditional bust of Jefferson on the obverse, the cheekbone is one of the high points to check for wear. On all examples, also check for detail in the hair and nice, clean surfaces with a minimum of scratches.

On the traditional reverse depiction of Monticello, the steps have long been a focal point. Look for sharp, clearly defined steps leading up to the building's entrance.

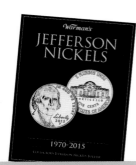

CHECK THE STEPS ON MONTICELLO

HOW TO STORE THEM

Folders provide suitable, handy, and attractive storage for Westward Journey 5-cent pieces obtained in circulation. The 2-by-2 holders are also practical alternatives if desired.

WARMAN'S JEFFERSON NICKELS 1970-2015 FOLDER

STILL THE SAME

Except for the war years of 1942-1945, the U.S. nickel 5-cent coin has been struck in the same size (21.2 millimeters), weight (5 grams), and composition (copper-nickel) since the Liberty nickel was introduced in 1883. That could change in the near future, however, as the U.S. Mint experiments with new coinage metals in response to the rising cost of copper.

LIBERTY NICKEL

WESTWARD JOURNEY NICKEL SERIES CHECKLIST

_____ 2004-P peace medal

_____ 2004-D peace medal

_____ 2004-P keelboat

_____ 2004-D keelboat

_____ 2005-P bison

_____ 2005-D bison

_____ 2005-P "Ocean in view!"

_____ 2005-D "Ocean in view!"

_____ 2006-P Monticello

_____ 2006-D Monticello

KNOW YOUR VALUES

Whenever searching bulk quantities of coins, have a value guide, such as the book *U.S. Coin Digest*, available for reference. This handy and easy-to-use reference lists the approximate retail values for coins.

Any older dates found should be checked in the guide to see if their values are above the norm. If they are, proper handling and storage methods should be followed to preserve the coins.

CHAPTER 5

COLLECTING THE BICENTENNIAL COINS

BICENTENNIAL QUARTER

There once was a time when a Bicentennial quarter was a common part of one's pocket change. But now, four decades after their release, Bicentennial coins, particularly the quarters, have become scarcer in circulating change.

With a little bit of effort, however, a nice set of Bicentennial coins can be put together for little cost. The resulting set provides a pleasing keepsake of our nation's 200th birthday.

THE STORY BEHIND THE COINS

A variety of coinage proposals for the nation's Bicentennial emerged in the years leading up to the celebration. Among them were proposals for special commemorative coins (the U.S. Mint had not issued commemorative coins since 1954), redesigning all six circulating coins, issuing a 2-cent coin with a Bicentennial design, and issuing a gold commemorative coin.

The Mint and Treasury Department initially resisted any changes to circulating coin designs and the issuance of commemorative coins, but they eased their opposition as the various proposals were winnowed to a final bill that was signed into law on October 18, 1973, by President Richard M. Nixon. That bill called for quarters, half dollars, and dollar coins struck after July 4, 1975, to bear new reverse designs emblematic of the nation's Bicentennial. The law also called for the coins to bear the dual date "1776-1976."

BICENTENNIAL HALF DOLLAR

BICENTENNIAL DOLLAR COIN

The law further authorized the Mint to strike the Bicentennial coins in a 40-percent silver composition (rather than the copper-nickel clad composition of the circulation strikes) for inclusion in three-coin uncirculated and proof sets for sale directly to collectors. The San Francisco Mint struck these special coins, which bear an "S" mintmark.

The San Francisco Mint also produced proof versions of all three coins in the circulating clad composition for inclusion in regular annual proof sets.

To select designs for the Bicentennial coins, the Mint sponsored a contest open to all U.S. citizens. The winners were announced in March 1974:

– A Revolutionary-era drummer-boy design, submitted by Jack L. Ahr of Arlington Heights, Illinois, was selected for the quarter.

– A depiction of Independence Hall, submitted by Seth G. Huntington of Minneapolis, was selected for the half dollar.

– A depiction of the Liberty Bell superimposed over the moon, submitted by Dennis R. Williams of Columbus, Ohio, was selected for the dollar. The moon was symbolic of the nation's lunar landings and exploration.

The Bicentennial coinage law gave the Treasury secretary the authority to determine how long the special reverse designs would be used. In September 1976, the Mint announced that Treasury Secretary William E. Simon had ordered the Mint to revert back to the old reverse designs with the beginning of 1977-dated coinage.

TWO CENTS WORTH

The proposal to strike a 2-cent coin for the nation's Bicentennial had precedent. The U.S. Mint issued circulating 2-cent coins in a copper-tin-zinc composition from 1864 through 1872. It also struck about 1,100 proof 2-cent pieces in 1873.

WHERE TO GET THEM

Bicentennial quarters still turn up occasionally in circulation, but not as often as they once did. A careful watch on pocket change should eventually produce an example.

Five rolls of quarters acquired from a local bank (200 coins total) turned up just one example, with a "D" mintmark. The same rolls produced two 1965-dated quarters and two 1966-dated quarters. The presence of the older coins in higher numbers may indicate that more people are putting aside the Bicentennial quarters as they encounter them in circulation. Also, more people are paying closer attention to the quarters in their pocket change thanks to the 50 State Quarters, District of Columbia and U.S. Territories Quarters, and the America the Beautiful Quarters.

BICENTENNIAL QUARTER

1965 QUARTER

1966 QUARTER

ROLLS OF QUARTERS

ROLLS OF HALF DOLLARS

Although the Mint still strikes half dollars for circulation, few of the big, bulky coins are actually used. Thus, rolls may be the best bet for acquiring Bicentennial half dollars from circulation. A five-roll sample (100 coins total) from a local bank yielded 10 Bicentennial half dollars, all with a "D" mintmark.

Even bigger and bulkier are the Eisenhower dollars with the Bicentennial reverse designs. The Eisenhower dollar was struck from 1971 to 1978; it was replaced by the smaller Anthony dollar in 1979.

That makes the Eisenhower dollar an obsolete design in a coin denomination that has never been popular among the public. A collector may be able to find a bank here and there that still has some.

A better bet, however, is a local coin shop or show. Nice examples in uncirculated grades should be available at either for just a few dollars each. They also give new collectors a low-cost introduction to buying coins over the counter.

Local shops and shows are also good sources for nice examples of the Bicentennial quarters and half dollars. Examples plucked from circulation will be well worn; a little extra money spent on purchased examples will produce a much nicer set.

Expect to find the 40 percent-silver proof and uncirculated sets at shops and shows, too. According to the book *U.S. Coin Digest*, the Bicentennial three-coin uncirculated set sells for about $20 and the Bicentennial three-coin proof set sells for about $25.

MINTMARKS

All three denominations of Bicentennial coins have either no mintmark, indicating they were struck at Philadelphia, or a "D" mintmark for Denver. Special collector versions struck for uncirculated and proof sets, including the 40-percent-silver versions, have an "S" mintmark for San Francisco.

BICENTENNIAL QUARTER MINTMARK DETAIL

On the quarter, the mintmark is on the obverse just behind the bow in Washington's hair on the lower right. On the half dollar, the mintmark is on the obverse just below Kennedy's neck. On the dollar, it's on the obverse just below Eisenhower's neck.

BICENTENNIAL DOLLAR IN 2-BY-2 HOLDER

BICENTENNIAL HALF DOLLAR IN 2-BY-2 HOLDER

BICENTENNIAL QUARTER IN 2-BY-2 HOLDER

CONDITION

On the quarter, Washington's cheek and the hair around his ear are key points to check for wear. On the half dollar, the cheek and hair are again key points. In particular, check for detail in the hair between the part in Kennedy's hair and his ear. On the dollar, Eisenhower's cheek and jawbone are also key points.

HOW TO STORE THEM

Folders are fine for Bicentennial coins plucked from circulation, but better examples purchased at shops and shows deserve a step up in storage systems. Nice examples of Bicentennial coins purchased individually at shows or shops will probably come in 2-by-2 holders. These are fine for long-term storage of these coins. So are hard-plastic holders, which can house coins either individually or as a set.

If you take purchased coins out of their 2-by-2 holders to transfer them to another storage system, observe all the rules for safe handling of coins:

– Handle them by the edges between your thumb and forefinger.
– Don't touch the obverse or reverse surfaces.
– Work over a soft surface.
– Be careful when removing coins from a 2-by-2 so the staples don't scratch the coin.
– Be equally careful when placing the coin into its new holder.

WHERE'S THE SHOW?

There's a coin show just about every weekend somewhere in the country. They range from mega-events, such as the American Numismatic Association's annual gatherings, to smaller one-day shows sponsored by local coin clubs.

To find a show near you, check the community events listings in your local newspaper. Or, pick up a copy of the monthly *Coins* magazine (available on most newsstands) or weekly *Numismatic News*. Each lists upcoming shows of all sizes held throughout the country.

BICENTENNIAL COIN SPECS

▷ **QUARTER (CIRCULATION STRIKES AND PROOF SETS):**

Obverse designer: John Flanagan.
Reverse designer: Jack L. Ahr.
Diameter: 24.3 millimeters.
Weight: 5.67 grams.
Composition: Clad layers of 75-percent copper and 25-percent nickel bonded to a pure-copper core.

▷ **QUARTER (SILVER UNCIRCULATED AND PROOF SETS):**

Weight: 5.75 grams.
Composition: Clad layers of 80-percent silver and 20-percent copper bonded to a core of 20.9-percent silver and 79.1-percent copper.
Total silver weight: 0.0739 troy ounces.

▷ **HALF DOLLAR (CIRCULATION STRIKES AND PROOF SETS):**

Obverse designer: Gilroy Roberts.
Reverse designer: Seth Huntington.
Diameter: 30.6 millimeters
Weight: 12.5 grams.
Composition: Clad layers of 75-percent copper and 25-percent nickel bonded to a pure copper core.

▷ **HALF DOLLAR (SILVER UNCIRCULATED AND PROOF SETS):**

Weight: 11.5 grams.
Composition: 40-percent silver, 60-percent copper.
Total silver weight: 0.148 troy ounces.

▷ **DOLLAR (CIRCULATION STRIKES AND PROOF SETS):**

Obverse designer: Frank Gasparro.
Reverse designer: Dennis R. Williams.
Diameter: 38.1 millimeters.
Weight: 22.68 grams.
Composition: 75-percent copper and 25-percent nickel bonded to a pure-copper core.

▷ **DOLLAR (SILVER UNCIRCULATED AND PROOF SETS):**

Weight: 24.59 grams.
Composition: Clad layers of 80-percent silver and 20-percent copper bonded to a core of 20.9-percent silver and 79.1-percent copper.
Total silver weight: 0.3161 troy ounces.

BICENTENNIAL COINAGE CHECKLIST

CIRCULATION STRIKES:

_____ 1976 quarter

_____ 1976-D quarter

_____ 1976 half dollar

_____ 1976-D half dollar

_____ 1976 dollar

_____ 1976-D dollar

SILVER UNCIRCULATED AND PROOF SETS:

_____ 1976-S uncirculated quarter

_____ 1976-S proof quarter

_____ 1976-S uncirculated half dollar

_____ 1976-S proof half dollar

_____ 1976-S uncirculated dollar

_____ 1976-S proof dollar

TYPE 1 AND TYPE 2 DOLLARS

Two styles of lettering appear on the reverse of the Eisenhower Bicentennial dollar coins with the clad composition – both circulation strikes and proofs. Bicentennial dollars struck in 1976 use thinner letters in "United States of America" and "One Dollar" than those struck in 1975 (but still dual-dated 1776-1976).

Coins with the earlier, fatter letters are referred to as Type 1; those with the later, thinner letters are referred to as Type 2. The Type 1 examples sell for slightly more at shops and shows.

The 40-percent silver versions do not have the design variation.

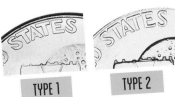

TYPE 1   TYPE 2

BICENTENNIAL COINAGE MINTAGES

CIRCULATION STRIKES

DATE, MINT MARK	DENOMINATION	MINTAGE
1976	Quarter	809,784,016
1976-D	Quarter	860,118,839
1976	Half dollar	234,308,000
1976-D	Half dollar	287,565,248
1976	Dollar	117,337,000
1976-D	Dollar	103,228,274

PROOFS, CLAD COMPOSITION

DATE, MINT MARK	DENOMINATION	MINTAGE
1976-S	Quarter	4,149,730
1976-S	Half dollar	7,059,099
1976-S	Dollar	7,059,099

UNCIRCULATED SETS, SILVER COMPOSITION

DATE, MINT MARK	DENOMINATION	MINTAGE
1976-S	Quarter	4,908,319
1976-S	Half dollar	4,908,319
1976-S	Dollar	4,908,319

PROOF SETS, SILVER COMPOSITION

DATE, MINT MARK	DENOMINATION	MINTAGE
1976-S	Quarter	3,998,621
1976-S	Half dollar	3,998,621
1976-S	Dollar	3,998,621

CHAPTER 6

COLLECTING THE 50 STATE QUARTERS

DISTRICT OF COLUMBIA AND U.S. TERRITORIES QUARTERS, AND AMERICA THE BEAUTIFUL QUARTERS

The 50 State Quarters program is the most successful mass-collecting opportunity in U.S. Mint history. The Mint once estimated that 147 million people collected the coins.

Upon completing its run, the program also spawned circulating quarters commemorating the District of Columbia and five U.S. territories in 2009, and national parks and other national sites beginning in 2010. The three programs combined give new collectors an excellent opportunity to build sets from circulation.

THE STORY BEHIND THE COINS

President Bill Clinton signed the 50 States Commemorative Coin Program Act into law on December 1, 1997. The bill originated in the Senate. It was introduced to "honor the unique Federal republic of 50 States that comprise the United States" and to "promote the diffusion of knowledge among the youth of the United States about the individual States, their history and geography, and the rich diversity of the national heritage."

The bill provided that from 1999 through 2008, the quarter's reverse would be redesigned to honor each of the 50 states. Five new designs would be introduced each year, and each new design would honor a different state. The states would be honored in the order in which they ratified the Constitution or were admitted to the union.

The bill gave authority for final approval of the designs to the Treasury secretary. It required the secretary to consult with each state's governor or the governor's designee on the respective state's

design. The designs were also reviewed by the U.S. Mint, the Citizens Coinage Advisory Committee, and the Commission of Fine Arts before the secretary's final approval.

The law banned any "frivolous or inappropriate" design. It further prohibited the depiction of a head-and-shoulders bust of any person, living or dead, or any representation of a living person.

To accommodate the reverse designs, the words "United States of America" were moved from the quarter's reverse to its obverse, and the date was moved from the obverse to the reverse. The traditional bust of George Washington, used on the quarter since 1932, was retained for the obverse of each coin.

The law also authorized the Mint to produce uncirculated and proof examples of the 50 State Quarters for sale to collectors and to produce examples in 90-percent-silver composition for sale to collectors.

QUARTERS SPECS

CLAD COMPOSITION

Diameter: 24.3 millimeters.

Weight: 5.67 grams.

Composition: Clad layers of 75-percent copper and 25-percent nickel bonded to a pure-copper core.

SILVER COMPOSITION

Diameter: 24.3 millimeters.

Weight: 6.25 grams.

Composition: 90-percent silver, 10-percent copper.

Total silver weight: 0.1808 troy ounces.

Legislation authorizing the District of Columbia and U.S. Territories Quarters was part of the 2008 Consolidated Appropriations Act, signed into law by President George W. Bush. Similar to the 50 State Quarters, the legislation required the Treasury secretary to consult with the chief executive of the District of Columbia and each of the five U.S. territories on the respective designs.

Each of the chief executives submitted two to three design narratives to the Treasury secretary. U.S. Mint designers created design proposals from the narratives. The proposals were reviewed by the Commission of Fine Arts and the Citizens Coinage Advisory Committee. The Treasury secretary had final design approval. Again similar to the 50 State Quarters, the authorizing legislation forbid any frivolous or inappropriate design, a depiction of a living person, or a head-and-shoulders image of any person living or dead. The traditional bust of George Washington was retained for the obverse of each coin.

The coins were released in two-month intervals beginning with the District of Columbia quarter in February 2009. It was followed, in order, by the coins honoring Puerto Rico, Guam, American Samoa, U.S. Virgin Islands, and the Northern Mariana Islands.

As with the 50 State Quarters, the legislation authorized the Mint to strike uncirculated, proof, and 90-percent silver versions for sale to collectors.

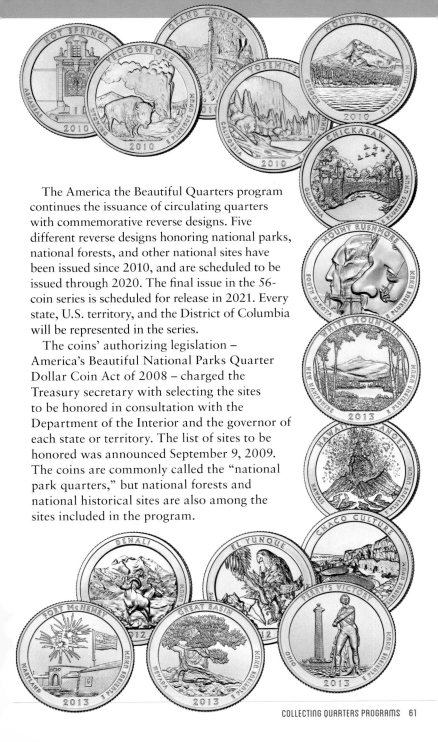

The America the Beautiful Quarters program continues the issuance of circulating quarters with commemorative reverse designs. Five different reverse designs honoring national parks, national forests, and other national sites have been issued since 2010, and are scheduled to be issued through 2020. The final issue in the 56-coin series is scheduled for release in 2021. Every state, U.S. territory, and the District of Columbia will be represented in the series.

The coins' authorizing legislation – America's Beautiful National Parks Quarter Dollar Coin Act of 2008 – charged the Treasury secretary with selecting the sites to be honored in consultation with the Department of the Interior and the governor of each state or territory. The list of sites to be honored was announced September 9, 2009. The coins are commonly called the "national park quarters," but national forests and national historical sites are also among the sites included in the program.

Like legislation for the state and territories quarters, the national sites legislation prohibits a head-and-shoulders depiction of any person living or dead, or a depiction of any living person. It also prohibits an outline or map of a state in the designs. The bust of George Washington continues to be used on the America the Beautiful Quarters obverses.

The legislation again authorizes the issuance of uncirculated, proof, and 90-percent-silver versions of the coins for sale to collectors.

Before the end of the series' ninth year, the Treasury secretary can decide to continue the series by honoring a second site in each state, territory, and the District of Columbia.

MINTMARKS

Circulation strikes for all of the quarters programs are produced at the Philadelphia ("P" mintmark) and Denver ("D" mintmark) mints. Special collector versions – for inclusion in uncirculated and proof sets, and the 90-percent-silver examples – are produced by the San Francisco Mint and carry an "S" mintmark.

The mintmark on the quarters is located on the obverse behind the bow in Washington's hair and below the words "In God We Trust." It is approximately the same location for the mintmark on quarters used since 1968.

WHERE TO GET THEM

A close watch on pocket change can quickly fill holes in a 50 State Quarters folder and may be the most fun way to collect the series. One collector filled about half of the 100 holes in his folder in about a year's time just from pocket change.

If you find a duplicate of a coin already in your folder, keep the one in better condition.

Searching rolls or other sources of bulk change can again speed the process. Six rolls of quarters (240 coins) obtained from a local bank yielded 62 of the 100 date and mintmark combinations ("P" and "D" example of each coin) required to complete a set of 50 State Quarters. Forty-four different states were represented, which

ROLLS OF QUARTERS

would put a collector well on his or her way to filling a folder that required just one example of each issue, regardless of mintmark.

Unfortunately, the sample rolls were not as productive for the District of Columbia and U.S. Territories Quarters and the America the Beautiful Quarters. Among the former, they yielded only one example each of the Guam and Puerto Rico issues, both with "D" mintmarks. There were no examples of the America the Beautiful Quarters in the rolls.

The District of Columbia and U.S. Territories Quarters and the America the Beautiful Quarters had the misfortune of being released just as the country was entering the depths of the Great Recession. The recession decreased demand for fresh coinage in the nation's economy, which lowered production of the new coins.

Mintages for the 50 State Quarters, for example, range from a low of 43 million for the 2000-P Virginia issue to a high of 194.6 million for the 2008-D Oklahoma issue. Most mintages range from 250 million to 300 million for the 2002-2008 issues.

Mintages for the 2009 District of Columbia and U.S. Territories Quarters range from a low of 35.2 million for the 2009-P Northern Mariana Islands issue to a high of 88.8 million for the 2009-D District of Columbia issue.

For the first year of the America the Beautiful Quarters (2010), mintages averaged 34.7 million. Figures were similar for the first four issues of the program's second year before starting to pick-up with the final issue of 2011, honoring the Chickasaw National Recreation Area. The Philadelphia Mint produced 73.8 million Chickasaw quarters and the Denver Mint produced 69.4 million.

Production dropped off again for the first three issues of 2012. Mintages ranged from a low of 21.6 million for the 2012-D Acadia

National Park quarter to a high of 25.8 million for the 2012-P El Yunque National Forest quarter. They rebounded with the final two issues of 2012. Philadelphia produced 46.2 million Hawai'i Volcanoes National Park quarters and Denver produced 78.6 million. Philadelphia produced 135.4 million Denali National Park quarters and Denver produced 166.6 million.

Quarters dated 2009-2012 may be a tougher find in circulation, but still, there are millions of them out there. They may come out of hiding if economic recovery increases demand for fresh coinage. Persistence and patience should eventually pay off for those intent on collecting them from circulation.

For those who aren't, nice examples from the various quarters programs can be purchased at coin shops and shows for a small premium. Uncirculated and proof versions, including the 90-percent-silver versions, of current-year issues can be purchased directly from the U.S. Mint (www.usmint.gov). Issues from previous years also can be purchased at shops and shows, or through coin-collecting publications.

CONDITION

On the obverse, Washington's cheek and the hair around his ear remain key points to check for wear on examples from the various quarters programs. Because of the wide variety of designs, it is difficult to pinpoint specific areas to check on reverses. In general, check detailed areas in the designs and look for a minimum of scratches and other surface abrasions.

HOW TO STORE THEM

Folders provide adequate, inexpensive, and handy storage for quarters collected from circulation. For purchased coins, 2-by-2 holders or an album in which both sides of the coin are protected are recommended. Follow all the rules for safe handling of coins (see Chapter 1) when transferring purchased coins from one storage method to another.

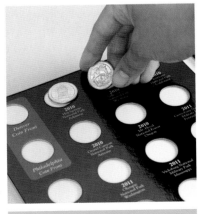

HAND PLACING A QUARTER IN A FOLDER

50 STATE QUARTERS CHECKLIST

▶ CIRCULATION STRIKES

_____ 1999-P Delaware

_____ 1999-D Delaware

_____ 1999-P Pennsylvania

_____ 1999-D Pennsylvania

_____ 1999-P New Jersey

_____ 1999-D New Jersey

_____ 1999-P Georgia

_____ 1999-D Georgia

_____ 1999-P Connecticut

_____ 1999-D Connecticut

_____ 2000-P Massachusetts

_____ 2000-D Massachusetts

_____ 2000-P Maryland

_____ 2000-D Maryland

_____ 2000-P South Carolina

_____ 2000-D South Carolina

_____ 2000-P New Hampshire

_____ 2000-D New Hampshire

_____ 2000-P Virginia

_____ 2000-D Virginia

_____ 2001-P New York

_____ 2001-D New York

_____ 2001-P North Carolina

_____ 2001-D North Carolina

THEY'RE OFFICIAL

The terms "50 State Quarters" and "America the Beautiful Quarters" are registered trademarks of the U.S. Mint.

_____ 2001-P Rhode Island

_____ 2001-D Rhode Island

_____ 2001-P Vermont

_____ 2001-D Vermont

_____ 2001-P Kentucky

_____ 2001-D Kentucky

_____ 2002-P Tennessee

_____ 2002-D Tennessee

_____ 2002-P Ohio

_____ 2002-D Ohio

_____ 2002-P Louisiana

_____ 2002-D Louisiana

_____ 2002-P Indiana

_____ 2002-D Indiana

_____ 2002-P Mississippi

_____ 2002-D Mississippi

_____ 2003-P Illinois

_____ 2003-D Illinois

_____ 2003-P Alabama

_____ 2003-D Alabama

_____ 2003-P Maine

_____ 2003-D Maine

_____ 2003-P Missouri

_____ 2003-D Missouri

_____ 2003-P Arkansas

_____ 2003-D Arkansas

_____ 2004-P Michigan

_____ 2004-D Michigan

_____ 2004-P Florida

_____ 2004-D Florida

_____ 2004-P Texas

_____ 2004-D Texas

_____ 2004-P Iowa

_____ 2004-D Iowa

_____ 2004-P Wisconsin

_____ 2004-D Wisconsin

_____ 2005-P Minnesota

_____ 2005-D Minnesota

_____ 2005-P Oregon

_____ 2005-D Oregon

_____ 2005-P Kansas

_____ 2005-D Kansas

_____ 2005-P West Virginia

_____ 2005-D West Virginia

_____ 2005-P California

_____ 2005-D California

_____ 2006-P Nevada

_____ 2006-D Nevada

_____ 2006-P Nebraska

_____ 2006-D Nebraska

_____ 2006-P Colorado

_____ 2006-D Colorado

_____ 2006-P North Dakota

_____ 2006-D North Dakota

_____ 2006-P South Dakota

_____ 2006-D South Dakota

_____ 2007-P Montana

_____ 2007-D Montana

_____ 2007-P Washington

_____ 2007-D Washington

_____ 2007-P Idaho

_____ 2007-D Idaho

_____ 2007-P Wyoming

_____ 2007-D Wyoming

_____ 2007-P Utah

_____ 2007-D Utah

_____ 2008-P Oklahoma

_____ 2008-D Oklahoma

_____ 2008-P New Mexico

_____ 2008-D New Mexico

_____ 2008-P Arizona

_____ 2008-D Arizona

_____ 2008-P Alaska

_____ 2008-D Alaska

_____ 2008-P Hawaii

_____ 2008-D Hawaii

HOW THEY BECAME TERRITORIES

The five territories honored on the 2009 quarters took varying paths to becoming part of the United States.

After centuries of Spanish rule, Puerto Rico was ceded to the United States under terms of the 1898 Treaty of Paris, which ended the Spanish-American War. It was designated a U.S. territory in 1917 and a U.S. commonwealth in 1952.

Guam also was ceded to the United States under the 1898 Treaty of Paris. It was originally placed under the U.S. Navy's administration, but it transferred to the Department of Interior when Guam was designated a territory in 1950.

American Samoa became part of the country as the result of an 1899 treaty among the United States, Great Britain, and Germany, all of whom had colonial and strategic interests in the region in the late 19th century. American Samoa should not be confused with independent Samoa (formerly known as Western Samoa), which lies just to the west of the U.S. territory.

The United States purchased the U.S. Virgin Islands from Denmark in 1917 for $25 million in gold coin under provisions of a treaty between the two countries signed in 1916. The islands were formerly known as the Danish West Indies.

The Northern Mariana Islands did not officially become a U.S. territory until 1976. Germany purchased the islands from Spain in 1899. Japan forced out Germany's colonial government in 1914. Japan's rule ended in 1944 when U.S. forces captured the islands during World War II. After the war, they became part of the United Nations' Trust Territory of the Pacific Islands under U.S. administration. In 1975, the Northern Marianas people voted to become a U.S. commonwealth, and the covenant took effect the following year.

In general, each territory has its own government, similar to a state government, which manages its internal affairs. The federal U.S. government is responsible for the territory's external affairs, such as trade, defense, and foreign relations.

The territories' residents are U.S. citizens but cannot vote in general presidential elections. They can vote in presidential primary elections. Each territory also elects one non-voting member to the U.S. House of Representatives.

DISTRICT OF COLUMBIA AND
U.S. TERRITORIES QUARTERS CHECKLIST

▶ **CIRCULATION STRIKES**

_____ 2009-P District of Columbia

_____ 2009-D District of Columbia

_____ 2009-P Puerto Rico

_____ 2009-D Puerto Rico

_____ 2009-P Guam

_____ 2009-D Guam

_____ 2009-P American Samoa

_____ 2009-D American Samoa

_____ 2009-P U.S. Virgin Islands

_____ 2009-D U.S. Virgin Islands

_____ 2009-P Northern Mariana Islands

_____ 2009-D Northern Mariana Islands

DISTRICT OF COLUMBIA
AND U.S. TERRITORIES
QUARTERS

AMERICA THE BEAUTIFUL QUARTERS

▶ CIRCULATION STRIKES

_____ 2010-P Hot Springs National Park (Arkansas)

_____ 2010-D Hot Springs National Park

_____ 2010-P Yellowstone National Park (Wyoming)

_____ 2010-D Yellowstone National Park

_____ 2010-P Yosemite National Park (California)

_____ 2010-D Yosemite National Park

_____ 2010-P Grand Canyon National Park (Arizona)

_____ 2010-D Grand Canyon National Park

_____ 2010-P Mount Hood National Forest (Oregon)

_____ 2010-D Mount Hood National Forest

_____ 2011-P Gettysburg National Military Park (Pennsylvania)

_____ 2011-D Gettysburg National Military Park

_____ 2011-P Glacier National Park (Montana)

_____ 2011-D Glacier National Park

_____ 2011-P Olympic National Park (Washington)

_____ 2011-D Olympic National Park

_____ 2011-P Vicksburg National Military Park (Mississippi)

_____ 2011-D Vicksburg National Military Park

_____ 2011-P Chickasaw National Recreation Area (Oklahoma)

_____ 2011-D Chickasaw National Recreation Area

THE FIRST AND OLDEST NATIONAL PARKS

An official history of Hot Springs National Park says the Arkansas site is America's "oldest national park." The official Web site for Yellowstone National Park says the Wyoming site is "America's first national park."

Which is correct? Both are, under the semantics employed above. Hot Springs National Park came under federal protection in 1832, a full 40 years ahead of Yellowstone. It was called a "federal reservation" at first; it was officially designated a "national park" in

_____ 2012-P El Yunque National Forest (Puerto Rico)

_____ 2012-D El Yunque National Forest

_____ 2012-P Chaco Culture National Historical Park (New Mexico)

_____ 2012-D Chaco Culture National Historical Park

_____ 2012-P Acadia National Park (Maine)

_____ 2012-D Acadia National Park

_____ 2012-P Hawai'i Volcanoes National Park (Hawaii)

_____ 2012-D Hawai'i Volcanoes National Park

_____ 2012-P Denali National Park (Alaska)

_____ 2012-D Denali National Park

_____ 2013-P White Mountain National Forest (New Hampshire)

_____ 2013-D White Mountain National Forest

_____ 2013-P Perry's Victory and International Peace Memorial (Ohio)

_____ 2013-D Perry's Victory and International Peace Memorial

_____ 2013-P Great Basin National Park (Nevada)

_____ 2013-D Great Basin National Park

_____ 2013-P Fort McHenry National Monument
and Historic Shrine (Maryland)

_____ 2013-D Fort McHenry National Monument and Historic Shrine

_____ 2013-P Mount Rushmore National Memorial (South Dakota)

_____ 2013-D Mount Rushmore National Memorial

1921. Based on the 1832 date, Hot Springs is America's "oldest national park" and thus was the subject of the first issue in the America the Beautiful Quarters program.

Yellowstone was immediately called a "national park," the first federal site to be so named, when it came under federal protection in 1872. Thus, Yellowstone can properly claim to be "America's first national park," though it had to settle for the second issue in the America the Beautiful Quarters program.

▶ SCHEDULED

2014 Great Smokey Mountains National Park (Tennessee)

2014 Shenandoah National Park (Virginia)

2014 Arches National Park (Utah)

2014 Great Sand Dunes National Park (Colorado)

2014 Everglades National Park (Florida)

2015 Homestead National Monument of America (Nebraska)

2015 Kisatchie National Forest (Louisiana)

2015 Blue Ridge Parkway (North Carolina)

2015 Bombay Hook National Wildlife Refuge (Delaware)

2015 Saratoga National Historical Park (New York)

2016 Shawnee National Forest (Illinois)

2016 Cumberland Gap National Historical Park (Kentucky)

2016 Harpers Ferry National Historical Park (West Virginia)

2016 Theodore Roosevelt National Park (North Dakota)

2016 Fort Moultrie (Fort Sumter National Monument) (South Carolina)

2017 Effigy Mounds National Monument (Iowa)

2017 Frederick Douglass National Historic Site (District of Columbia)

2017 Ozark National Scenic Riverways (Missouri)

2017 Ellis Island National Monument (Statue of Liberty) (New Jersey)

2017 George Rogers Clark National Historic Park (Indiana)

2018 Pictured Rocks National Lakeshore (Michigan)

2018 Apostle Islands National Lakeshore (Wisconsin)

2018 Voyageurs National Park (Minnesota)

2018 Cumberland Island National Seashore (Georgia)

2018 Block Island National Wildlife Refuge (Rhode Island)

2019 Lowell National Historical Park (Massachusetts)

2019 American Memorial Park (Northern Mariana Islands)

2019 War in the Pacific National Historical Park (Guam)

2019 San Antonio Missions National Historical Park (Texas)

2019 Frank Church-River of No Return Wilderness (Idaho)

2020 National Park of American Samoa (American Samoa)

2020 Weir Farm National Historic Site (Connecticut)

2020 Salt River Bay National Historical Park and Ecological Preserve
     (U.S. Virgin Islands)

2020 Marsh-Billings-Rockefeller National Historical Park (Vermont)

2020 Tallgrass Prairie National Preserve (Kansas)

2021 Tuskegee Airmen National Historic Site (Alabama)

CHAPTER 7

COLLECTING FRANKLIN HALF DOLLARS

Franklin half dollars are an excellent choice for collectors looking to take the next step after collecting coins from circulation. They offer many virtues as a first series to collect through buying:

– All of the issues in the series are now more than 50 years old.

– They were struck in the traditional 90-percent silver composition and contain more than a third of a troy ounce of precious metal.

– They are big, making them easy to examine and grade.

– Examples are readily available at shows, shops, and through advertisements in coin-collecting publications.

– The series is long (1948-1963), making for a significant accomplishment when a collection is completed. But it is not so long that completing it is excessively challenging.

– Nice examples in higher circulated grades or even lower uncirculated grades are affordable.

THE STORY BEHIND THE COIN

Mint Director Nellie Tayloe Ross was apparently the driving force behind the change from the Walking Liberty half dollar to the Franklin half dollar in 1948. Some collectors may consider the switch an artistic faux pas. Adolph A. Weinman's Walking Liberty design is considered a classic in U.S. coinage history. John R. Sinnock's staid bust of Franklin is technically sound but not as aesthetically pleasing.

Ross, however, had wanted to introduce a coin honoring Benjamin Franklin for some time. A U.S. Mint news release (dated January 7, 1948) announcing the new coin says, "Mrs. Ross envisaged several years ago a new half dollar honoring Franklin and the Liberty Bell."

WALKING LIBERTY HALF DOLLAR

Only the Treasury secretary had to approve the design change because the Walking Liberty half dollar, introduced in 1916, had been used for more than 25 years.

According to some historical accounts, Ross also considered changing the cent's design to depict Franklin because of his saying "A penny saved is twopence clear," which morphed into "A penny saved is a penny earned." But she chose the half dollar instead because the larger silver coin allowed for a better image of Franklin.

Sinnock's bust of Franklin on the obverse is a "composite study of Franklin's face in full profile," the Mint's 1948 news release says. It was based on a variety of Franklin portraits, the Mint said. The Liberty Bell depiction on the reverse is based on the 1926 U.S. Sesquicentennial commemorative half dollar, also designed by Sinnock.

DEATH OF AN ENGRAVER

John Sinnock, the Mint engraver who designed the Franklin half dollar, never saw his Franklin design on a production coin. Sinnock died in 1947, after completing work on the design but before production of the coin began.

1954 FRANKLIN HALF DOLLAR

WHERE TO GET THEM

It's possible a well-worn Franklin half dollar could still turn up in a roll of half dollars or another source for bulk change. But the chances that the big coin in a denomination that isn't popular in circulation could get through without being put aside at some point are slim.

Thus, coin shops, shows, and advertisements in coin-collecting publications are the best sources for collectible Franklin half dollars. They are commonly found through all three.

HOW MUCH?

Expect to pay about $15 per coin for Franklin half dollars in upper circulated or lower uncirculated grades. Precious-metals markets have been volatile in recent years, so fluctuations in silver prices can affect the base value of Franklin half dollars.

Expect to pay more for some key dates. They include the 1949-D, 1949-S, 1952-S, and 1955. Franklin half dollars in upper uncirculated grades can sell for hundreds or even thousands of dollars. The book *U.S. Coin Digest* values the 1953-S in grade MS-65 with full lines on the lower part of the Liberty Bell at $16,000.

MINTMARKS

Franklin half dollars have either no mintmark, indicating they were struck at the Philadelphia Mint; a "D" mintmark for Denver; or an "S" mintmark for San Francisco. The "S" mintmark was used in only five years: 1949 and 1951-1954.

The mintmark appears on the reverse, above the wooden beam holding the Liberty Bell.

MINTMARK
DETAIL

CONDITION

On the obverse, the high point of Franklin's cheek and the hair around his ear are key areas to check for wear. On the reverse, check the straps holding the bell to the beam and the lettering on the bell itself.

Uncirculated examples with full lines running across the bottom of the bell command substantial premiums. These are often listed as "MS-65FBL" in value guides, meaning a coin grading MS-65 with "full bell lines."

THE WHAT HALF DOLLAR?

Some value guides may list a 1955 "Bugs Bunny" Franklin half dollar. An obverse die was damaged in coin production that year, apparently when it was struck in the coining press by a reverse die without a blank coin in between.

As subsequent coins were struck by the damaged die, Franklin's upper lip was split, giving him the appearance of having large front teeth like the cartoon character for which the variety is nicknamed.

The variety sells for a small premium over regular 1955 Franklin half dollars but is not required for a collection of the series to be regarded as complete.

HOW TO STORE THEM

Franklin half dollars purchased through shows, shops, or advertisements should be stored in 2-by-2 holders or an album that protects both sides of the coin. When it's necessary to handle a coin outside of a holder, follow all the rules outlined in Chapter 1 for safe handling of coins.

SPECS

FRANKLIN HALF DOLLAR SPECS

Designer: John R. Sinnock.

Diameter: 30.6 millimeters.

Weight: 12.5 grams.

Composition: 90-percent silver, 10-percent copper.

Total silver weight: 0.3618 troy ounces.

FRANKLIN HALF DOLLAR CHECKLIST

_____ 1948

_____ 1948-D

_____ 1949

_____ 1949-D

_____ 1949-S

_____ 1950

_____ 1950-D

_____ 1951

_____ 1951-D

_____ 1951-S

_____ 1952

_____ 1952-D

_____ 1952-S

_____ 1953

_____ 1953-D

_____ 1953-S

_____ 1954

_____ 1954-D

_____ 1954-S

_____ 1955

_____ 1956

_____ 1957

_____ 1957-D

_____ 1958

_____ 1958-D

_____ 1959

_____ 1959-D

_____ 1960

_____ 1960-D

_____ 1961

_____ 1961-D

_____ 1962

_____ 1962-D

_____ 1963

_____ 1963-D

WHAT'S A TROY OUNCE?

Silver and gold are weighed in troy ounces. A troy ounce (31.103 grams) is slightly heavier than an avoirdupois ounce (28.350 grams). Twelve troy ounces equal one troy pound.

The term originated in the city of Troyes, France, whose medieval fairs set the standards for European weights and measures.

CHAPTER 8

COLLECTING KENNEDY HALF DOLLARS

1964 KENNEDY HALF DOLLAR

Now in its sixth decade, the Kennedy half dollar series spans several milestones in U.S. coinage history:

– The first issues, dated 1964, were struck in the traditional 90-percent-silver composition.

– From 1965 through 1970, they were struck in a 40-percent-silver composition that is unique among circulating U.S. coins.

– Since 1971, they have been struck in the copper-nickel clad composition used for other circulating U.S. coins.

– As noted in Chapter 5, the Kennedy half dollar was also part of the Bicentennial coinage series struck in 1975 and 1976 with special reverses and the dual dates "1776-1976."

THE STORY BEHIND THE COIN

It was only days after John F. Kennedy's assassination on November 22, 1963, when proposals to honor the slain president on a coin emerged. The quarter, half dollar, and dollar were all considered before the half dollar was chosen.

President Lyndon Johnson announced his support for honoring Kennedy on the half dollar in a news release on December 10, 1963. Congressional approval was required because the Franklin half dollar design had been used for less than 25 years.

Johnson and many in Congress wanted the new coin approved quickly so production could begin with the new year's coinage in January 1964. That would avoid having half dollars of two different designs (Franklin and Kennedy) struck in the same year and thus avoid the added expense of having to prepare dies for two different designs in the same year.

Congressional approval did indeed come quickly. President Johnson signed the bill authorizing the Kennedy half dollar on December 30, 1963.

U.S. Mint documents, however, reveal that Mint engravers were advised of a probable Kennedy coin as early as late November 1963. The Mint's chief engraver, Gilroy Roberts, said Mint Director Eva Adams notified him of the probable change "shortly after" Kennedy's assassination. "A day or so later, about November 27th, Miss Adams called again and informed me that the Half dollar had been chosen for the new design," Roberts said in his written recollection of the time. Roberts further related that the president's widow, Jacqueline Kennedy, did not want to replace the image of George Washington on the quarter with her late husband's image.

KENNEDY PRESIDENTIAL MEDAL

Thus, work on the Kennedy half dollar began at the Mint before the authorizing legislation was signed into law. To accommodate the tight turnaround time from concept to production, it was decided to adapt artwork already in-house. Kennedy's portrait on the obverse and the presidential seal on the reverse were both based on his official presidential medal. Roberts had designed the medal's obverse, so he worked on adapting it for the half dollar. His assistant engraver, Frank Gasparro, who later succeeded Roberts as chief engraver, had designed the medal's reverse, so he worked on adapting it for the half dollar.

They apparently worked quickly, because trial strikes were made December 13, more than two weeks before President Johnson signed the authorizing legislation. Regular production of the Kennedy half dollar began simultaneously at the Philadelphia and Denver mints at 11 a.m. Eastern time on February 11, 1964.

Adams expected the two mints combined to strike 90 million Kennedy half dollars in 1964, about the same number of Franklin half dollars struck in 1963. But demand for the new coin was so great that 1964 production at the two mints combined topped 433 million.

THE PRESIDENTS WIDOW APPROVES

Among those who reviewed the Kennedy half-dollar design before it entered production was the president's widow, Jacqueline Kennedy. "Mrs. Kennedy was favorably impressed with the design on both sides of the coin," Mint chief engraver Gilroy Roberts later recalled, "but felt it would be an improvement if the part in the hair, on the portrait, was less pronounced and more accents were added."

Roberts said the suggested changes were made before production began.

"They also had in mind a design showing a full figure or half figure of the late President," Roberts said. "There was simply not enough time to create new designs and medals, get approvals, etc. and have the new coin in production by January, 1964. I strongly advocated the simplicity and directness of a profile portrait as being the best possible arrangement for a handsome, outstanding coin whose beauty would endure and there could be no doubt as to the identity of the subject."

WHERE TO GET THEM

Several strategies can be used to collect Kennedy half dollars because of their long run and the aforementioned variety in composition. Collectors, therefore, may want to focus on just one segment of the series at a time. When that segment is complete, they can move on to another.

Following is a series breakdown:

▶ 1964

It's possible that a 1964 Kennedy half dollar may still turn up in pocket change or rolls, but the chances of one of the 90-percent-silver coins going undetected through circulation all these years are small. Thus, shops and shows are the best bets for acquiring one. Expect to pay about $15 for a nice example in a lower uncirculated grade. Base prices for silver Kennedy half dollars may fluctuate with the precious-metals markets.

1964 KENNEDY HALF DOLLAR

WHY NO 1975 HALF DOLLARS?

Kennedy half dollars struck in 1975 and 1976 carried the special Bicentennial reverse design and were all dated "1776-1976."

1965 KENNEDY HALF DOLLAR

▶ 1965-1970

The 40-percent-silver issues may have a slightly better chance of slipping through in circulation, but five rolls of half dollars (100 coins) obtained from a local bank yielded none. So shows and shops are the places to go again. About $6 each should buy pleasing examples in lower circulated grades. Again, base prices for 1965-1970 Kennedy half dollars may fluctuate with the precious-metals markets.

▶ 1971-DATE

Circulating coinage – be it pocket change, rolls from banks, or other sources of bulk change – is a good source for circulated examples of these base-metal issues. Coins from the five-roll sample mentioned above filled 20 of 48 holes in a Warman's folder for half dollars dated 1964 through 1986. (The folder included spots for coins originally available only in special collector sets from the U.S. Mint.) The oldest was a 1971-D.

Look to shows or shops for better examples in lower uncirculated grades, especially for the older issues. Expect to pay $1 to $2 apiece.

► MINTMARKS

Kennedy half dollars with no mintmark were struck at the Philadelphia Mint. A "P" mintmark began appearing on Philadelphia strikes in 1980. A "D" mintmark

indicates the Denver Mint. Proofs and other special versions struck specially for sale directly to collectors through the years were struck at the San Francisco Mint and carry an "S" mintmark.

On 1964 Kennedy half dollars, the mintmark is located on the reverse below the eagle's right claw. From 1968 to the present, it is located on the obverse between Kennedy's neck and the date.

► CONDITION

Kennedy's cheek and hair are key points to check for wear on the obverse. In particular, check for detail in the hair between the part in Kennedy's hair and his ear. On the reverse, the eagle's tail feathers are key points.

► HOW TO STORE THEM

Folders for Kennedy half dollars are available and provide adequate storage for coins collected from circulation. Uncirculated coins – those purchased at shows or shops – should be stored in 2-by-2 holders or albums in which both sides of the coin are protected. If it is necessary to handle an uncirculated Kennedy half dollar, follow the rules for safe handling of coins outlined in Chapter 1.

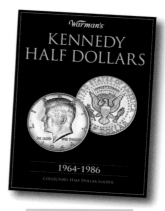

WARMAN'S FOLDER
FOR 1964-1986
KENNEDY HALF DOLLARS

KENNEDY HALF DOLLAR SPECS

Obverse designer: Gilroy Roberts.
Reverse designer: Frank Gasparro.
Diameter: 30.6 millimeters.

▶ 1964

Weight: 12.5 grams.
Composition: 90-percent silver, 10-percent copper.
Total silver weight: 0.3618 troy ounces.

▶ 1965-1970

Weight: 11.5 grams.
Composition: clad layers of 80-percent silver and 20-percent copper bonded to a core of 20.9-percent silver and 79.1-percent copper.
Total silver weight: 0.148 troy ounces.

▶ 1971-DATE

Weight: 11.34 grams.
Composition: clad layers of 75-percent copper and 25-percent nickel bonded to a pure-copper core.

THE SILVER HALF LIVES ON

In 1992 the U.S. Mint resumed production of the traditional 90-percent silver half dollars, but they are included in annual uncirculated and proof sets only, not for circulation. All are produced at the San Francisco Mint and have an "S" mintmark.

Collectors can purchase current-year sets directly from the Mint. Sets from previous years are available on the secondary market, such as coin shops and shows.

KENNEDY HALF-DOLLAR CHECKLIST

CIRCULATION STRIKES

_____ 1964	_____ 1983-P
_____ 1964-D	_____ 1983-D
_____ 1965	_____ 1984-P
_____ 1966	_____ 1984-D
_____ 1967	_____ 1985-P
_____ 1968-D	_____ 1985-D
_____ 1969-D	_____ 1986-P
_____ 1971	_____ 1986-D
_____ 1971-D	_____ 1987-P
_____ 1972	_____ 1987-D
_____ 1972-D	_____ 1988-P
_____ 1973	_____ 1988-D
_____ 1973-D	_____ 1989-P
_____ 1974	_____ 1989-D
_____ 1974-D	_____ 1990-P
_____ 1976	_____ 1990-D
_____ 1976-D	_____ 1991-P
_____ 1977	_____ 1991-D
_____ 1977-D	_____ 1992-P
_____ 1978	_____ 1992-D
_____ 1978-D	_____ 1993-P
_____ 1979	_____ 1993-D
_____ 1979-D	_____ 1994-P
_____ 1980-P	_____ 1994-D
_____ 1980-D	_____ 1995-P
_____ 1981-P	_____ 1995-D
_____ 1981-D	_____ 1996-P
_____ 1982-P	_____ 1996-D
_____ 1982-D	_____ 1997-P

_____	1997-D	_____	2006-P
_____	1998-P	_____	2006-D
_____	1998-D	_____	2007-P
_____	1999-P	_____	2007-D
_____	1999-D	_____	2008-P
_____	2000-P	_____	2008-D
_____	2000-D	_____	2009-P
_____	2001-P	_____	2009-D
_____	2001-D	_____	2010-P
_____	2002-P	_____	2010-D
_____	2002-D	_____	2011-P
_____	2003-P	_____	2011-D
_____	2003-D	_____	2012-P
_____	2004-P	_____	2012-D
_____	2004-D	_____	2013-P
_____	2005-P	_____	2013-D
_____	2005-D		*Series is ongoing.*

2004-S PROOF KENNEDY HALF DOLLAR

WHY NO 1970 HALF DOLLARS?

In 1970 the U.S. Mint struck Kennedy half dollars for inclusion in uncirculated and proof sets only. None was struck for circulation.

The 40-percent-silver half dollars struck for circulation from 1965 through 1969 were the only U.S. precious-metal coins remaining in circulation. The public hoarded them, resulting in chronic shortages of the denomination.

The Mint suspended circulation production of the half dollar for 1970 until Congress authorized a change to the clad composition used for the circulating dime and quarter.

The 1970 half dollars struck for uncirculated sets that year were produced at Denver and have a "D" mintmark. The proof versions were struck at San Francisco and have an "S" mintmark.

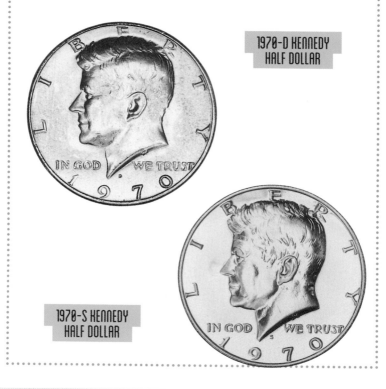

1970-D KENNEDY
HALF DOLLAR

1970-S KENNEDY
HALF DOLLAR

CHAPTER 9

COLLECTING EISENHOWER DOLLARS

1971-D EISENHOWER DOLLAR

The Eisenhower dollar continued the 20th-century trend of honoring deceased presidents on coins. It is the last of the large (38.1 millimeters in diameter) dollar coins, but unfortunately for the former World War II general and later president, the denomination and size have never been popular for a circulating coin. Thus, the series was short-lived (1971-1978).

Collectors today, however, still value the series for its subject and the very bulk that made it unpopular in circulation. Its short run also makes it an easy and affordable series to complete. Some special collector issues struck in silver are an optional bonus to a collection of Ike dollars, as they are commonly called in the hobby.

THE STORY BEHIND THE COIN

Dwight D. Eisenhower, supreme commander of the Allied forces in Europe during World War II and the 34th U.S. president, died March 28, 1969. Legislation to again strike a dollar coin, which had not been produced since 1935, was introduced in Congress the following fall. It provided that Eisenhower be honored on the dollar's obverse. The reverse was to be emblematic of the first moon landing, which occurred July 21, 1969.

Honoring Eisenhower apparently wasn't the sole motivation for the legislation. Several historical accounts say Nevada casino interests pushed for the United States to again strike a dollar coin.

The legislation did not become law until the last day of December 1970. But like the Kennedy half dollar, U.S. Mint engravers began work on the new coin's design well before the legislation was approved.

Mint chief sculptor and engraver Frank Gasparro designed both sides of the coin. He started work on the obverse in spring 1969 and on the reverse the following fall.

Mint documents say Gasparro's obverse design was inspired by his attendance at a welcome-home and victory parade in

MINT PROFILE: SAN FRANCISCO

The San Francisco branch mint was authorized in 1852 to bring coin production closer to bullion sources. S-mint coinage commenced in 1854 but stopped in 1955. It resumed again in 1968, largely to  produce proof and other special versions of coins for sale directly to collectors, such as the 40-percent-silver Eisenhower dollars. Over the years, San Francisco has produced a wide range of base-metal, silver, and gold coinage.

Eisenhower's honor on June 20, 1945, in New York City. Then a junior engraver at the Mint, Gasparro had a curbside view of the parade on Fifth Avenue.

"Mr. Gasparro got only a fleeting glimpse of the Supreme Commander of the Allied Armies in Europe as he rode by," the Mint documents say. "He carried his image of Eisenhower's courage and character back to work with him at the Philadelphia Mint and immediately made a profile drawing suitable to cut directly in steel and capture the strong facial features that so deeply impressed him."

Twenty-four years later, Gasparro referred back to his 1945 drawings and other Eisenhower portraits when he began work on the dollar coin.

For the reverse, Gasparro fashioned an eagle with an olive branch, a symbol of peace, in its claws landing on the moon with the Earth symbolized as a small orb in the background. The Apollo 11 spacecraft that first landed on the moon was nicknamed "The Eagle."

Trial strikes were made January 21, 1971, at the Philadelphia Mint, but circulation production did not begin until late fall of that year. All circulation coins were struck in the clad composition.

The Eisenhower dollar legislation also authorized the production of 40-percent-silver specimens for inclusion in uncirculated and proof sets. Production of these special collector versions began March 31, 1971, at the San Francisco Mint. The 40-percent-silver Ike dollars were also produced from 1972 through 1974 in uncirculated and proof versions, and again in 1975 and 1976 with the Bicentennial reverse.

MAKING MONEY

In 1971, the San Francisco Mint's four coining presses could produce a total of 240,000 uncirculated Eisenhower dollars in an eight-hour shift.

MAMIE APPROVED

As was the case with the Kennedy half dollar, the widow of the president depicted on the coin was allowed to review and approve the Eisenhower dollar before it entered production. The U.S. Mint reported that Mamie Eisenhower was "especially pleased with the portrait of her late husband."

WHERE TO GET THEM

Because of their obsolete size, Eisenhower dollars rarely turn up in circulation. A bank here or there may still have a rare roll of them or other small supply stuck in a drawer somewhere. Like the Kennedy half dollars, the coins were also hoarded by some when new, so an individual stash or two may surface.

Ike dollars, however, are commonly found at shows and shops, which are the best sources for completing a collection of nice examples.

1974-D EISENHOWER DOLLAR

SPECS

EISENHOWER DOLLAR SPECS

Designer: Frank Gasparro

Diameter: 38.1 millimeters.

Circulation strikes

Weight: 22.68 grams.

Composition: 75-percent copper and 25-percent nickel bonded to a pure copper core.

UNCIRCULATED AND PROOF SETS

Weight: 24.59 grams.

Composition: clad layers of 80-percent silver and 20-percent copper bonded to a core of 20.9-percent silver and 79.1-percent copper.

Total silver weight: 0.3161 troy ounces.

HOW MUCH?

Expect to pay about $5 to $10 for a nice uncirculated example of a circulation strike in the clad composition. Exceptions are the 1973, 1973-D, and 1974. The 1973 and 1973-D have mintages of only 2 million each. Expect to pay $10 to $15 for either of the 1973 circulation versions. The 1974 has the next-lowest mintage among circulation strikes at 27.3 million and sells for about $15 in uncirculated grades.

The 40-percent-silver versions of 1971-1974 are slightly more – about $16 for those originally issued in uncirculated sets, depending on silver bullion prices. According to the book *U.S. Coin Digest*, most of the proof versions of the same years range up to $20. The 1973-S proof is the most expensive at about $45.

MINTMARKS

Circulating Eisenhower dollars have either no mintmark, indicating they were struck at Philadelphia, or a "D" mintmark for Denver. The 40-percent-silver versions were struck at San Francisco and have an "S" mintmark.

The mintmark appears on the obverse below Eisenhower's neck and above the date.

CONDITION

High points on the obverse to check for wear are Eisenhower's cheekbone and jaw line. On the reverse, check for detail in the eagle's head and wing feathers.

HOW TO STORE THEM

Uncirculated and proof versions of Eisenhower dollars purchased at shops and shows should be stored in 2-by-2 holders or an album in which both sides of the coins are protected. Follow all the rules outlined in Chapter 1 for safe handling of coins.

A PEACEFUL EAGLE

According to U.S. Mint documents, Mint officials were concerned about the characterization of the eagle on the Eisenhower dollar's reverse. Mint Director Mary Brooks instructed designer Frank Gasparro to fashion a "peaceful eagle." Gasparro described the resulting depiction as a "pleasant-looking eagle."

EISENHOWER DOLLAR CHECKLIST

▶ CLAD COMPOSITION

_____ 1971

_____ 1971-D

_____ 1972

_____ 1972-D

_____ 1973

_____ 1973-D

_____ 1973-S (proofs only)

_____ 1974

_____ 1974-D

_____ 1974-S (proofs only)

_____ 1976

_____ 1976-D

_____ 1976-S (proofs only)

_____ 1977

_____ 1977-D

_____ 1977-S (proofs only)

_____ 1978

_____ 1978-D

_____ 1978-S (proofs only)

1972-S PROOF
EISENHOWER DOLLAR

▶ 40-PERCENT-SILVER COMPOSITION

Uncirculated versions were struck for inclusion in uncirculated sets; proof versions were struck for inclusion in proof sets.

_____ 1971-S uncirculated

_____ 1971-S proof

_____ 1972-S uncirculated

_____ 1972-S proof

_____ 1973-S uncirculated

_____ 1973-S proof

_____ 1974-S uncirculated

_____ 1974-S proof

_____ 1976-S uncirculated

_____ 1976-S proof

A TRUE SILVER DOLLAR

Circulating dollar coins of clad composition are often referred to as "silver" dollars, but the term should be reserved for dollar coins that actually contain the precious metal.

The traditional silver dollars of the 1800s were composed of 90-percent-silver and contain 0.7736 troy ounces of the precious metal. The last circulating U.S. silver dollar was struck in 1935.

The 40-percent- silver versions of the Eisenhower dollars, because they contain some of the precious metal, can truly be called silver dollars. The clad-composition coins struck for circulation, however, should not be called silver dollars.

1921 SILVER DOLLAR

CHAPTER 10

COLLECTING NATIVE AMERICAN DOLLARS

2009 AGRICULTURE

2010 GREAT TREE OF PEACE

The U.S. government put a new twist on its long-running battle to get Americans to use dollar coins when it introduced the Native American series in 2009. Like their predecessors, the Native American dollar coins have not seen widespread use in everyday commerce. But they have created another collectible series that is readily available with a little bit of effort.

THE STORY BEHIND THE COINS

Despite their popularity with collectors today, the traditional large dollar coin (38.1 millimeters in diameter) was never popular in circulation. The public preferred a thin, light dollar bill to the heavy, bulky dollar coin. Thus, the Eisenhower dollar in the traditional size (see Chapter 9) suffered the same commercial fate as its silver predecessors a century earlier.

The U.S. government attempted to reverse the public's rejection of circulating dollar coins when it authorized a new, smaller dollar coin (26.5 millimeters in diameter) in legislation signed into law by President Jimmy Carter on October 10, 1978. The law specified that the coin's obverse honor 19th-century women's activist Susan B. Anthony (1820-1906).

On paper, a smaller dollar coin makes sense. It costs more to produce than a dollar bill, but it lasts longer in circulation, thus saving the government money in the long run.

But in practice, the Anthony dollar initially suffered the same commercial fate as its larger predecessors. The major reason was its similarity in size to the quarter, which is 24.3 millimeters in diameter. The two were often confused, and people sometimes spent the dollar coin while believing they were spending a quarter.

The new dollar coin was released into circulation on July 2, 1979, in Anthony's hometown of Rochester, New York. Through 1980, the U.S. Mint struck more than 847 million Anthony dollars, but by 1981, many of them sat in Mint storage because

1979 ANTHONY DOLLAR

banks were not ordering them. Thus, the Mint struck 1981-dated Anthony dollars for uncirculated and proof sets only and stopped production altogether after 1981.

In the 1990s, however, mass-transit organizations and the vending-machine industry started drawing down the government's inventory of Anthony dollars as their automated systems started accepting the higher denomination. On May 20, 1999, the Mint announced that it would strike 1999-dated Anthony dollars for circulation to meet demand until production of the new Sacagawea dollar coin could begin in 2000. The Mint struck more than 41 million 1999 Anthony dollars.

President Bill Clinton signed into law the U.S. Coin Act of 1997 on December 1 of that year. It mandated that a new, golden-colored dollar coin be struck to replace the Anthony dollar.

SACAGAWEA DOLLAR

Besides the color, the law also mandated that the coin have a "distinctive edge" as opposed to the reeded edge of the Anthony dollar and Washington quarter. It also has a wider border than other circulating coins. All of these features were incorporated into the new coin to try to distinguish it from the quarter and answer a major criticism of the Anthony dollar.

The law did not, however, mandate a design theme for the coin. That was left to Treasury Secretary Robert E. Rubin, who created the Dollar Coin Design Advisory Committee to lead the process. With public input, the citizen panel eventually recommended a design featuring Sacagawea, the Native American woman who accompanied Lewis & Clark on their exploration of the American West. She gave birth during the journey, so she is depicted with her child on her back.

As the design selection process proceeded, U.S. Mint officials met quarterly with representatives from transit authorities, the vending-machine industry, the banking business, retail businesses, and others with an interest in the coin's success. All of this was an effort to make the new coin right where the old Anthony dollar went wrong.

The coin was released into commerce in January 2000. The following March, the Mint launched a marketing campaign, also mandated by the authorizing legislation, to increase awareness and promote acceptance of the new coin. The campaign cost $40 million, all of which came from Mint operating revenues, not tax dollars, according to the Mint.

Initially, it appeared the pre-production planning and marketing campaign paid off. The Mint said it produced and shipped more than 500 million Sacagawea dollars by the end of April 2000. In all, it produced more than 1.28 billion 2000-dated Sacagawea dollar coins for circulation.

2011 DIPLOMACY, TREATIES WITH TRIBAL NATIONS

By the following year, however, production fell to more than 133 million circulation strikes. From 2002 through 2007, circulation-strike production averaged just 7.36 million annually. It rebounded a bit in 2008, when the Philadelphia Mint struck 9.8 million Sacagawea dollars and the Denver Mint struck 14.84 million.

Congress passed a law in 2007 mandating that the reverse of the Sacagawea dollar coin be changed each year beginning in 2009 to celebrate the contributions of Indian tribes and individual Native Americans to the country's development and history. The law mandates that Native American dollars make up at least 20 percent of the U.S. Mint's annual production of Native American and Presidential dollars (see Chapter 11) combined.

The coins' obverses continue to depict Sacagawea. The date of issue, mintmark, and motto "E Pluribus Unum" appear as incused lettering on the edges.

THE SCULPTOR'S MODEL

Sculptor Glenna Goodacre used a Shoshone college student, Randy'L Hedow Teton, as her model for the depiction of Sacagawea on the obverse of the dollar coin. The child Sacagawea is carrying on her back is a depiction of her son Jean Baptiste. Sacagawea was six months pregnant when she joined Lewis & Clark's expedition, and the child was born early in the journey. Goodacre also designed the Vietnam Women's Memorial in Washington, D.C.

NATIVE AMERICAN DOLLAR SPECS

Obverse designer: Glenna Goodacre.

Reverse designers: Norman E. Nemeth (2009), Thomas Cleveland (2010, 2012), Richard Masters (2011), Susan Gamble (2013).

Diameter: 26.4 millimeters.

Weight: 8.07 grams.

Composition: 88.5-percent copper, 6-percent zinc, 3.5-percent manganese, 2-percent nickel.

The U.S. Mint consults with the Senate Committee on Indian Affairs, House of Representatives Congressional Native American Caucus, National Congress of American Indians, U.S. Commission of Fine Arts, and the Citizens Coinage Advisory Committee in determining future designs. The Treasury secretary has final authority in the selection process.

2012 17TH-CENTURY TRADE ROUTES

Through 2013, the U.S. Mint had released the following coins in the series:

▶ 2009 AGRICULTURE

The design depicts a Native American woman planting seeds. The design is a tribute to the tradition and importance of agriculture in Native American culture.

▶ 2010 GREAT TREE OF PEACE

The design depicts the Hiawatha Belt, which symbolizes the five Native American nations that made up the Iroquois Confederacy. The central figure on the belt, a great white pine, symbolizes the Onondaga Nation. The four squares flanking it represent the Mohawk, Oneida, Cayuga, and Seneca nations.

▶ 2011 DIPLOMACY, TREATIES WITH TRIBAL NATIONS

The design depicts the hands of Supreme Sachem Ousamequin Massasoit and Governor John Carver symbolically offering a ceremonial peace pipe after the first formal peace alliance between the Wampanoag tribe and European settlers was finalized in 1621.

▶ 2012 17TH CENTURY TRADE ROUTES

The design depicts a Native American man and a horse, with horses running in the background.

▶ 2013 DELAWARE TREATY

After declaring its independence, the United States signed its first formal treaty with an Indian tribe, the Delaware, on September 17, 1778, at Fort Pitt (now Pittsburgh). The design depicts a turkey, a howling wolf, and a turtle – all symbols of various Delaware clans – and 13 stars in a ring to represent the original Colonies.

WHERE TO GET THEM

Because dollar coins are seldom used in everyday transactions, rolls from banks are the best sources for collecting Native American dollars from circulation. Four rolls (100 coins) obtained from a local bank yielded examples of the 2009, 2010, and 2011 issues – all with "D" mintmarks.

The U.S. Mint sells current-year issues in uncirculated and proof sets, and in rolls. Uncirculated and proof versions from previous years are available at coin shops and shows.

CHEERIOS COINS

Cereal boxes have contained many trinkets over the years to try to entice buyers, especially kids. So the U.S. Mint turned to this traditional marketing gimmick when introducing the Sacagawea dollar in 2000.

During the coin's launch, Sacagawea dollars were inserted into 11 million boxes of General Mills' Cheerios. Buyers of the brand had a 1-in-2,000 chance of finding one of the coins in their purchased box.

"Advertising experts have estimated that the Cheerios campaign brought the Mint the equivalent of 132 million advertising impressions," the Mint reported in March 2001.

MINTMARKS

Native American dollars struck for circulation have either a "P" mintmark for Philadelphia or a "D" mintmark for Denver. Proof versions have an "S" mintmark for San Francisco.

As previously noted, the date and mintmark appear on the edge of a Native American dollar. A magnifying glass can be helpful for, first, finding the mintmark and, second, deciphering it.

CONDITION

On the obverse, check for wear on the high point of Sacagawea's cheekbone and for detail in her hair and her child's hair. Key points on the reverses can vary depending on the design, but in general, check for wear on the design's high points and in its details.

HOW TO STORE THEM

Folders are fine for coins collected from circulation. Purchased coins should remain in their original U.S. Mint packaging or in 2-by-2 or hard-plastic holders.

NATIVE AMERICAN DOLLAR CHECKLIST

▶ **CIRCULATION STRIKES**

_____ 2009-P

_____ 2009-D

_____ 2010-P

_____ 2010-D

_____ 2011-P

_____ 2011-D

_____ 2012-P

_____ 2012-D

_____ 2013-P

_____ 2013-D

Series is ongoing.

2013 DELAWARE TREATY

CHAPTER 11

COLLECTING PRESIDENTIAL DOLLARS

I f it worked for quarters, it should work for dollar coins. That was the reasoning behind the introduction of the Presidential dollar-coin series in 2007. Unfortunately, the four new reverse designs issued annually in the series have done nothing to make a circulating dollar coin more popular. For collectors, however, the series offers a fun and educational opportunity – with a catch.

COMMON OBVERSE DESIGN FOR PRESIDENTIAL DOLLARS

THE STORY BEHIND THE COINS

The Presidential dollars series was yet another attempt to get Americans to use dollar coins instead of dollar bills. The authorizing legislation – the Presidential $1 Coin Act of 2005 – cites a Government Accountability Office study that says Americans would use dollar coins if they were issued with attractive, educational, and rotating designs, like the 50 State Quarters. The law mandates that federal agencies and agencies that receive federal funds, such as some transit authorities, take the necessary steps to ensure that they are capable of receiving and dispensing the coins.

But in December 2011, Treasury Secretary Timothy F. Geithner announced that the U.S. Mint was suspending the production of Presidential dollars for circulation because of a large backlog of inventory. Geithner said collectors could continue to purchase future issues in the series from the Mint.

Four presidents are scheduled to be honored each year through 2015 in the order in which they served. The program is scheduled to conclude in 2016 with issues honoring Richard M. Nixon and Gerald Ford. The law specifies that a former or current president cannot be added to the series while he is still alive or within two years of his death.

The law mandates that the coins' obverses depict a likeness of the president being honored, his name, a number indicating the order in which he served, and the years of his term or terms. Grover Cleveland, the only president to serve two non-consecutive

EDGE LETTERING ON PRESIDENTIAL DOLLARS

terms (1885-1889 and 1893-1897), appears on two separate coins in 2012 as the 22nd and 24th president.

The law designates that the common reverse design be a depiction of the Statue of Liberty.

To make more room for the obverse and reverse designs, the original law specified that each coin's date of issue, its mintmark, and the mottos "E Pluribus Unum" and "In God We Trust" appear as incused lettering on the

THE CASE OF THE MISSING EDGE LETTERING

A number of early Presidential dollars escaped the U.S. Mint without their edge lettering. According to *Numismatic News* error-coin expert Ken Potter, hundreds of thousands of George Washington dollars may have been released without the edge lettering, along with 10,000-15,000 John Adams dollars and an estimated 1,500 Thomas Jefferson dollars.

In the early days of Presidential-dollar production, the coins were taken in bins from the coining presses to a separate machine that applied the edge lettering. Apparently, not all of the coins made the trip from the coining press to the edge-lettering machine and were released into circulation without the edge lettering.

Since then, the edge-lettering process has been incorporated into the regular production line, which has reduced the number of coins escaping without the edge lettering.

According to the book *U.S. Coin Digest*, a 2007 George Washington dollar without edge lettering is worth about $75 in uncirculated condition.

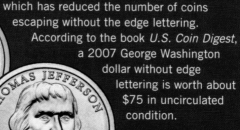

edge. A 2007 amendment requires that "In God We Trust" appear on the coins' obverse or reverse. "In God We Trust" appears on the obverse of the Presidential dollars beginning with the 2009 issues.

Presidential dollars are struck in the same specifications as the Sacagawea dollars, which have been produced since 2000 (see Chapter 10) and will continue to be produced in addition to the Presidential dollars.

WHERE TO GET THEM

Presidential dollars dated 2007-2011 can be collected through roll searches. A four-roll sample obtained from a local bank yielded an example of each president from the five-year period. Thus, a collector desiring just one example of each president, regardless of mintmark, could have a complete collection of 2007-2011 coins just from the sample rolls.

Denver Mint issues dominated the sample rolls, but a few Philadelphia issues were also found, which could start a collection that included an example of each circulating issue from each mint.

So what's the catch to collecting Presidential dollars? As noted above, the U.S. Mint stopped production of the coins for circulation in late 2011. It continued, however, to produce Presidential dollars for inclusion in uncirculated and proof sets. So Presidential dollars dated 2012 and later must be purchased unless the Mint resumes circulation production.

Current-year issues can be purchased directly from the Mint (www.usmint.gov). In 2013, the Mint offered Presidential dollars in various uncirculated and proof sets, and in rolls, bags, and boxes of various quantities. Prior-year issues can be purchased at coin shops and shows.

MINTMARKS

Presidential dollars struck for circulation and uncirculated sets have either a "P" mintmark for Philadelphia or a "D" mintmark for Denver. Proof issues have an "S" mintmark for San Francisco.

The mintmark appears on the edges of Presidential dollars. A magnifying glass is helpful for finding and then deciphering the mintmark.

IS THAT LETTERING UPSIDE DOWN?

No, there is no such thing as upside-down edge lettering on Presidential dollars or the Native American dollars (see chapter 10).

Automation feeds the coins through the edge-lettering machine is mass quantities. Sometimes the obverse may be facing up when the coin goes through; sometimes the reverse may be facing up when the coin goes through. Thus, there's no standard for which way the lettering will face when you turn a Presidential dollar to look at its edge.

Also, the coins can be turned different ways when they go through the edge-lettering machine. So there is no standard for the placement of the edge lettering relative to the obverse design. A coin's mintmark, for example, may be on the edge above the obverse portrait on one coin but below it on another.

This requires more effort on a collector's part to find the mintmarks when searching rolls of coins and can contribute to the early onset of eye fatigue. For that reason, collectors may want to limit themselves to a couple of rolls of Presidential dollars per search session.

CONDITION

In general, check for wear on the high points of the obverse design, such as the cheekbone in the portrait. Also check for wear in the design's details, such as the lines in the hair.

HOW TO STORE THEM

Folders are fine for Presidential dollars collected from circulation. Purchased coins should stay in their original U.S. Mint packaging or 2-by-2 or hard-plastic holders.

SPECS

PRESIDENTIAL DOLLAR SPECS

Diameter: 26.4 millimeters.

Weight: 8.07 grams.

Composition: 88.5-percent copper, 6-percent zinc, 3.5-percent manganese, 2-percent nickel.

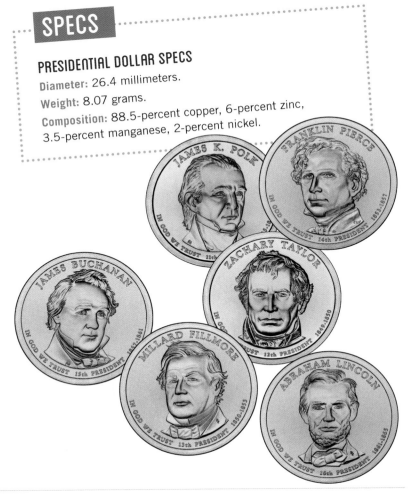

PRESIDENTIAL DOLLAR CHECKLIST

CIRCULATION STRIKES

_____ 2007-P George Washington

_____ 2007-D George Washington

_____ 2007-P John Adams

_____ 2007-D John Adams

_____ 2007-P Thomas Jefferson

_____ 2007-D Thomas Jefferson

_____ 2007-P James Madison

_____ 2007-D James Madison

_____ 2008-P James Monroe

_____ 2008-D James Monroe

_____ 2008-P John Quincy Adams

_____ 2008-D John Quincy Adams

_____ 2008-P Andrew Jackson

_____ 2008-D Andrew Jackson

_____ 2008-P Martin Van Buren

_____ 2008-D Martin Van Buren

_____ 2009-P William Henry Harrison

_____ 2009-D William Henry Harrison

_____ 2009-P John Tyler

_____ 2009-D John Tyler

_____ 2009-P James K. Polk

_____ 2009-D James K. Polk

_____ 2009-P Zachary Taylor

_____ 2009-D Zachary Taylor

_____ 2010-P Millard Fillmore

_____ 2010-D Millard Fillmore

_____ 2010-P Franklin Pierce

_____ 2010-D Franklin Pierce

_____ 2010-P James Buchanan

_____ 2010-D James Buchanan

_____ 2010-P Abraham Lincoln

_____ 2010-D Abraham Lincoln

_____ 2011-P Andrew Johnson

_____ 2011-D Andrew Johnson

_____ 2011-P Ulysses S. Grant

_____ 2011-D Ulysses S. Grant

_____ 2011-P Rutherford B. Hayes

_____ 2011-D Rutherford B. Hayes

_____ 2011-P James Garfield

_____ 2011-D James Garfield

STRUCK FOR UNCIRCULATED SETS ONLY

_____ 2012-P Chester A. Arthur

_____ 2012-D Chester A. Arthur

_____ 2012-P Grover Cleveland (first term)

_____ 2012-D Grover Cleveland (first term)

_____ 2012-P Benjamin Harrison

_____ 2012-D Benjamin Harrison

_____ 2012-P Grover Cleveland (second term)

_____ 2012-D Grover Cleveland (second term)

_____ 2013-P William McKinley

_____ 2013-D William McKinley

_____ 2013-P Theodore Roosevelt

_____ 2013-D Theodore Roosevelt

_____ 2013-P William Howard Taft

_____ 2013-D William Howard Taft

_____ 2013-P Woodrow Wilson

_____ 2013-D Woodrow Wilson

SCHEDULED

2014 William Harding

2014 Calvin Coolidge

2014 Herbert Hoover

2014 Franklin D. Roosevelt

2015 Harry S. Truman

2015 Dwight D. Eisenhower

2015 John F. Kennedy

2015 Lyndon B. Johnson

2016 Richard M. Nixon

2016 Gerald Ford

CHAPTER 12

COLLECTING MODERN U.S. COMMEMORATIVES

1982-S PROOF WASHINGTON HALF DOLLAR

Congress has authorized a myriad of commemorative coin series since 1982. Commemorative coins honor events, people, organizations, or things and are authorized by law. They are official U.S. government issues and legal tender, but they are not intended to circulate. Instead, they are sold directly to collectors by the U.S. Mint at a premium above face value. Laws authorizing commemorative coins usually mandate that a certain amount of the purchase price benefits a group or event related to the coin's theme.

In terms of cost, collecting modern commemoratives is a step up from collecting coins from circulation at face value or buying them at shops or shows for a few dollars each. But focusing on one or more collecting strategies, as outlined below, can keep purchases within a budget.

THE STORY BEHIND THE COINS

The first U.S. commemorative coin was an 1892 half dollar for the Columbian Exposition. The exposition was held May 1 through October 30, 1893, in Chicago to commemorate the 400th anniversary of Columbus' arrival in the New World. The U.S. Mint struck 950,000 Columbian half dollars dated 1892 and more than 1.5 million dated 1893.

1892 COLUMBIAN EXPOSITION HALF DOLLAR

The Columbian half dollar opened the door to many other commemorative coins from the 1910s and continuing into the 1950s. Most were silver half dollars, but there was also an 1893 quarter (also for the Columbian Exposition), a number of gold dollars, two gold $2.50 coins, and two gold $50 coins.

The coins were sold by the Mint at a premium above face value with a portion of the proceeds benefiting some organization or event related to the coin's theme. Some of the coins commemorated state anniversaries or national themes, such as the U.S. Sesquicentennial in 1926.

There were no less than 18 commemorative half dollars issued in 1936 alone. Among them was an issue commemorating the 75th anniversary of the Battle of Gettysburg. Others, however, were of little national importance, such as issues for the Cincinnati Music Center and the centennial of Elgin, Illinois.

CINCINNATI MUSIC CENTER HALF DOLLAR

Congress grew weary of U.S. coinage being used as local fundraisers, and the flow of commemorative coins slowed in the 1940s and '50s. The last issue among what are commonly called "early" commemoratives was a 1954 half dollar honoring Booker T. Washington and George Washington Carver.

WASHINGTON-CARVER HALF DOLLAR

A 28-year hiatus on commemorative coinage ensued until Congress authorized a half dollar in the traditional 90-percent-silver composition to honor the 250th anniversary of George Washington's birth in 1982. Thus began what are commonly called "modern" commemoratives.

The Washington coin was a winner in many respects: First, its theme was of truly national significance and worthy of commemoration. Second, its design by Mint engraver Elizabeth Jones featured a striking depiction of Washington on horseback, a departure from the staid busts used for portraiture on coins since the Lincoln cent of 1909. The reverse, also designed by Jones, features a view of Washington's Mount Vernon home.

These factors, combined with the long break in commemorative coinage, made the coin popular with collectors. The Mint sold more than 2.2 million uncirculated versions ("D" mintmark) and almost 4.9 million proof versions ("S" mintmark).

Like the Columbian half dollar 90 years earlier, the George Washington half dollar opened the door to more commemorative coinage, and like the commemorative coinage of the 1930s, an undesirable proliferation resulted. The coins' themes in the 1990s weren't as localized as many of those in the 1930s, but commemorative coinage became an easy mark for senators and U.S. representatives looking to do a favor for a constituency or a favor for a fellow lawmaker by offering their vote for a commemorative coin program. Commemorative coins could raise

ANCIENT ROOTS

Commemoratives have their roots in some of the world's first coins. Roman generals used their coinage privileges to strike issues commemorating their military conquests.

1994
COMMEMORATIVES

funds for a pet cause through surcharges on the Mint's sales of the coins, and a vote for a program went largely unnoticed by the general public.

The year 1994 alone brought five commemorative coin programs: World Cup soccer, National Prisoner of War Museum, U.S. Capitol Bicentennial, Vietnam Veterans Memorial, and Women in Military Service Memorial. Although each theme had its virtues, the market for commemorative coins couldn't keep up with all the issues, and sales plummeted from the highs of the Washington half dollar and other early issues in the modern era.

In response, Congress passed the Commemorative Coin Reform Act of 1996. Among other provisions, it limits the number of commemorative themes to two per year. In addition, congressional proposals for commemorative coins must be reviewed by the Citizens Coinage Advisory Committee, which reports to the Treasury secretary. The 10-person committee consists of members from the general public and those with credentials in American history, sculpture, and numismatics.

WHERE TO GET THEM

Current-year commemoratives can be purchased directly from the U.S. Mint (www.usmint.gov). Issues from previous years can be purchased at shows, shops, or through advertisements in hobby publications, such as *Coins* magazine.

COLLECTING STRATEGIES

A complete collection of every commemorative half dollar, silver dollar, and gold coin issued since 1982 is a commendable but daunting goal for many collectors, especially beginners. Following are suggestions for getting started in collecting modern commemoratives, which can lead to expanding the collection in the future:

▶ COLLECT WHAT YOU LIKE

If you see a modern commemorative coin and you like it, buy it. The coin may appeal to you because of its theme or design. Whatever the reason, if you like the coin and are willing to pay the asking price, it will make a great addition to your collection.

▶ BY DENOMINATION

A new collector may want to focus on just the commemorative half dollars issued since 1982 or just the silver dollars. With a good value guide in hand and more money to spend, a new collector could also venture into gold coins and select one or more of the many commemorative gold $5 and $10 coins.

1986-S STATUE OF LIBERTY CENTENNIAL SILVER DOLLAR

▶ BY THEME

Collectors of modern commemoratives can also focus on a particular theme that appeals to them, such as presidents, the Olympics or other sports, women, or military themes. Again, collect what you like.

1997-S JACKIE ROBINSON SILVER DOLLAR

1993-S THOMAS JEFFERSON SILVER DOLLAR

▶ AS A COMPLEMENT TO A CIRCULATING-COIN COLLECTION

One or more commemorative coins can complement a collection of circulating coins with similar design themes. For example, a 1993 silver dollar commemorating the 250th anniversary of Thomas Jefferson's birth can complement a collection of Westward Journey nickels (see Chapter 4). A 1990 silver dollar commemorating the centennial of Dwight Eisenhower's birth can complement a collection of Eisenhower dollars (see Chapter 9).

▶ BY SET

When selling a current-year commemorative series, the U.S. Mint often offers various sets containing individual coins in the series in uncirculated and proof versions. For example, the 1986 Statue of Liberty Centennial coin series consisted of a base-metal half dollar, silver dollar, and gold $5. Various sets of the series offered by the Mint that year included a two-coin set consisting of an uncirculated silver dollar and clad half dollar; a three-coin set consisting of uncirculated versions of each coin; and a six-coin set consisting of proof and uncirculated versions of each coin.

These and sets of other series can be found in their original Mint packaging at shops and shows, and through advertisements in hobby publications such as *Coins* magazine.

HOW MUCH?

Some of the least popular commemorative coins at the time of their issue are the most expensive on the secondary market today, and some of the most popular commemorative coins at the time of their issue are the most affordable today. Why? The least popular coins didn't sell as well, which resulted in lower mintages. Generally speaking, scarcer coins are more valued by collectors, which increases demand and drives up their asking prices on the secondary market.

For example, the 1982 George Washington silver commemorative half dollar was popular and sold well at the time of issue. With millions of coins produced, either an uncirculated or proof example can be purchased for under $15.

In contrast, less than 50,000 uncirculated versions of the 1996 Atlanta Olympics commemorative clad half dollar with the swimmer design were produced. Expect to pay more than $100 for one on the secondary market.

MINTMARKS

Modern U.S. commemorative coins have either a "P" mintmark for Philadelphia, "D" for Denver, "S" for San Francisco, or a "W" for West Point, New York. Mintmark location varies by coin.

CONDITION

Commemorative coins are specially handled and packaged at the mints. Thus, grading is less of a factor in purchasing and collecting them if they are still in their original Mint packaging.

Still, check each coin before you purchase it or after you receive it in the mail. Make sure its surfaces are clean and free of scratches or other significant blemishes.

The U.S. Mint has a 30-day return policy for coins purchased directly from it. Mail-order dealers, such as those who advertise in *Coins* magazine, also offer return policies. Check individual ads for specific terms.

HOW TO STORE THEM

Keep commemorative coins in their original U.S. Mint packaging, whether purchased directly from the Mint or on the secondary market. The packaging is suitable for long-term storage and protects the coins from wear and blemishes that occur when handled directly.

MODERN COMMEMORATIVE COIN SPECS

Commemorative coins are struck in traditional specifications for the denomination and composition. Future issues may be subject to change from the specs listed below.

▶ CLAD HALF DOLLARS

Diameter: 30.6 millimeters.

Weight: 11.34 grams.

Composition: clad layers of 75-percent copper and 25-percent nickel bonded to a pure-copper core.

▶ SILVER HALF DOLLARS

Diameter: 30.6 millimeters.

Weight: 12.5 grams.

Composition: 90-percent silver, 10-percent copper.

Actual silver weight: 0.3618 troy ounces.

▶ SILVER DOLLARS

Diameter: 38.1 millimeters.

Weight: 26.73 grams.

Composition: 90-percent silver, 10-percent copper.

Actual silver weight: 0.76 troy ounces.

▶ GOLD $5

Diameter: 21.5 millimeters.

Weight: 8.359 grams.

Composition: 90-percent gold, 10-percent alloy.

Actual gold weight: 0.24 troy ounces.

▶ GOLD $10

Diameter: 27 millimeters.

Weight: 26.73 grams.

Composition: 90 percent gold, 10 percent alloy.

Actual gold weight: 0.484 troy ounces.

CHECKLIST

All coins listed below were or are scheduled to be offered in proof and uncirculated versions.

► SILVER HALF DOLLARS

_____ 1982 George Washington 250th Anniversary of Birth

_____ 1993 James Madison, Father of the Bill of Rights

► CLAD HALF DOLLARS

_____ 1986 Statue of Liberty Centennial

_____ 1986 Bicentennial of the Congress

_____ 1991 Mount Rushmore Golden Anniversary

_____ 1991 World War II 50th Anniversary (struck in 1993)

_____ 1992 Olympics

_____ 1992 500th Anniversary of Columbus Discovery

_____ 1994 World Cup Soccer

_____ 1995 Atlanta Olympics (basketball design)

_____ 1995 Atlanta Olympics (baseball design)

_____ 1995 Civil War

_____ 1996 Atlanta Olympics (soccer design)

_____ 1996 Atlanta Olympics (swimmer design)

_____ 2001 U.S. Capitol Visitor Center

_____ 2003 First Flight Centennial

_____ 2008 Bald Eagle

_____ 2011 U.S. Army

_____ 2013 Five-Star Generals

_____ 2015 Baseball Hall of Fame

_____ 2015 U.S. Marshal Service
225th Anniversary

▶ SILVER DOLLARS

_____ 1983 Los Angeles XXII Olympiad

_____ 1984 Los Angeles XXII Olympiad

_____ 1986 Statue of Liberty Centennial

_____ 1987 The U.S. Constitution 200th Anniversary

_____ 1988 Olympiad

_____ 1989 Bicentennial of the Congress

_____ 1990 Eisenhower Centennial

_____ 1991 28th Anniversary Korea

_____ 1991 Mount Rushmore Golden Anniversary

_____ 1991 USO 50th Anniversary

_____ 1991-1995 World War II 50th Anniversary series (struck in 1993)

_____ 1992 Columbus Quincentenary

_____ 1992 Olympics

_____ 1992 The White House 1792-1992

_____ 1993 James Madison

_____ 1993 Thomas Jefferson 1743-1993

_____ 1994 National Prisoner of War Museum

_____ 1994 Bicentennial of United States Capitol

_____ 1994 Vietnam Veterans Memorial

_____ 1994 Women in Military Service Memorial

_____ 1994 World Cup 94

_____ 1995 Atlanta Olympics (gymnastics design)

_____ 1995 Atlanta Olympics (track and field design)

_____ 1995 Atlanta Olympics (cycling design)

_____ 1995 Atlanta Olympics (Paralympics design)

_____ 1995 Civil War

_____ 1995 Special Olympics World Games

_____ 1996 Atlanta Olympics (tennis design)

_____ 1996 Atlanta Olympics (rowing design)

_____ 1996 Atlanta Olympics (high jumper design)

_____ 1996 Atlanta Olympics (Paralympics design)

_____ 1996 National Community Service

_____ 1996 Smithsonian Institution 1846-1996

_____ 1997 Jackie Robinson 50th Anniversary

_____ 1997 National Law Enforcement Officers Memorial

_____ 1997 United States Botanic Garden 1820-1995

_____ 1998 Black Revolutionary War Patriots

_____ 1998 Robert F. Kennedy

_____ 1999 Dolley Madison

_____ 1999 Yellowstone National Park

_____ 2000 Leif Ericson

_____ 2000 Library of Congress 1800-2000

_____ 2001 American Buffalo

_____ 2001 U.S. Capitol 1800-2001

_____ 2002 West Point Bicentennial

_____ 2002 XIX Olympic Winter Games

_____ 2003 First Flight Centennial

_____ 2004 Thomas Alva Edison

_____ 2004 Lewis & Clark Bicentennial

_____ 2005 Chief Justice John Marshall

_____ 2005 Marines 1775-2005

_____ 2006 Benjamin Franklin
Tercentenary (Franklin portrait design)

_____ 2006 Benjamin Franklin Tercentenary
(kite flying design)

_____ 2006 San Francisco Old Mint

_____ 2007 Founding of Jamestown 1607-2007

_____ 2007 Little Rock High School Desegregation

_____ 2008 Bald Eagle

_____ 2009 Abraham Lincoln

_____ 2009 Louis Braille

_____ 2010 Disabled Veterans

_____ 2010 Boy Scouts of America 1910-2010

_____ 2011 Medal of Honor

_____ 2011 U.S. Army

_____ 2012 Star Spangled Banner Bicentennial

_____ 2012 U.S. Infantry

_____ 2013 Five-Star Generals

_____ 2013 Girl Scouts of America

_____ 2014 1964 Civil Rights Act

_____ 2015 Baseball Hall of Fame

_____ 2015 U.S. Marshal Service 225th Anniversary

_____ 2017 Lions Clubs International Centennial

▶ GOLD $5

_____ 1986 Statue of Liberty Centennial

_____ 1987 Bicentennial of the Constitution

_____ 1988 Olympiad

_____ 1989 Bicentennial of the Congress

_____ 1991 Mount Rushmore Golden Anniversary

_____ 1991-1995 World War II 50th Anniversary (struck in 1993)

_____ 1992 Columbus Quincentenary

_____ 1992 Olympics

_____ 1993 James Madison

_____ 1994 World Cup 94

_____ 1995 Civil War

_____ 1995 Atlanta Olympics
(torch-runner design)

_____ 1995 Atlanta Olympics (stadium design)

_____ 1996 Atlanta Olympics (cauldron design)

_____ 1996 Atlanta Olympics (flag-bearer design)

_____ 1996 Smithsonian Institution 1846-1996

_____ 1997 Franklin Delano Roosevelt

_____ 1997 Jackie Robinson
50th Anniversary

_____ 1999 George Washington
(bicentennial of death)

_____ 2001 U.S. Capitol 1801-2000

_____ 2002 XIX Olympic Winter Games

_____ 2006 San Francisco Old Mint

_____ 2007 Founding of Jamestown 1607-2007

_____ 2008 Bald Eagle

_____ 2011 Medal of Honor

_____ 2011 U.S. Army

_____ 2012 Star Spangled Banner Bicentennial

_____ 2013 Five-Star Generals

_____ 2015 Baseball Hall of Fame

_____ 2015 U.S. Marshal Service
225th Anniversary

▶ GOLD $10

_____ 1984 Los Angeles XXII Olympiad

_____ 2000 Library of Congress

_____ 2003 First Flight Centennial

CHAPTER 13

COLLECTING UNCIRCULATED AND PROOF SETS

1999 PROOF SET

Uncirculated and proof sets have a long tradition in U.S. Mint history and among collectors. They were created as a means for collectors to obtain pristine examples of current-year coinage. That tradition continues today with a wide variety of sets available from the Mint, which reflects the wide variety of current U.S. coinage.

THE STORY BEHIND THE COINS

Proof coins are struck from specially selected, highly polished planchets and dies. They usually receive multiple strikes from the coining press at increased pressure. The result is a coin with mirrorlike surfaces and, in recent years, a cameo effect on its raised design surfaces.

The coins are then carefully handled; placed in sealed, inert holders; and sold to collectors in sets. Traditionally, the sets contain one proof example of each coin struck for circulation that year (cent through dollar), but with the proliferation of commemorative coins and other special issues in recent years, such as the America the Beautiful Quarters, the Mint has offered multiple proof sets in a single year.

In 2012, for example, the Mint's proof-set offerings included a Presidential dollar set; a set that contained 90-percent silver examples of the dime, quarters, and half dollar; an America the Beautiful Quarters set; and an America the Beautiful Quarters silver set.

2007 PRESIDENTIAL DOLLARS PROOF SET

U.S. proof coins date back as early as 1795 but were struck largely as presentation pieces for VIPs. The Mint started selling sets to the general public in 1936. Proof sets were not produced from 1943 through 1949 and again from 1965 through 1967, but they have been offered continuously since 1968.

Like proof sets, uncirculated sets have traditionally contained one example of each coin struck for circulation in their year of issue, including one example of each mintmark for a particular denomination. Unlike proof sets, however, the coins in uncirculated sets are struck from production planchets and dies, and do not receive multiple strikes from the coining press, so they look more like their circulating counterparts than high-quality proof coins do.

Coins in uncirculated sets, also commonly called "mint sets," still receive special handling and packaging, so they are referred to as "uncirculated." They are sometimes removed from their original Mint packaging on the secondary market and sold individually.

THE NON-MINT UNCIRCULATED SETS

In years when the U.S. Mint did not offer uncirculated sets, some private companies compiled and marketed uncirculated sets. These privately produced and marketed sets still have collectible value depending on the scarcity and condition of their individual coins, but they should not be confused with the Mint's officially issued sets.

GRADING PROOF COINS

Because proof coins are struck by a special process, they receive their own grading designation. A coin does not start out being a proof and then become mint state if it becomes worn or damaged. Once a proof coin, always a proof coin.

The American Numismatic Association's official standards for grading proof coins assign designations proof-60 through proof-70 (proof-63, proof-65, and so on) to these specially produced coins in various condition. The ANA says a proof coin with many marks, dents, scratches, or other blemishes should be called an "impaired" proof.

These account for the individual uncirculated examples of late-date coins sold at shows and shops.

The Mint has sold uncirculated sets to the general public since 1947 with a couple of interruptions. For 1965, 1966, and 1967, the Mint did not produce proof sets or traditional uncirculated sets. Instead it marketed what it called "Special Mint Sets." Coins in the Special Mint Sets were of higher quality than the traditional uncirculated sets but were not up to proof-coin standards.

The Mint did not offer uncirculated sets in 1982 and 1983.

WHERE TO GET THEM

Current-year sets are available directly from the U.S. Mint (www.usmint.gov). Previous year's sets may be available directly from the Mint also if supplies last. For example, some 2012 sets were still available from the Mint in early 2013.

Past-year sets are available at shows, shops, or through advertisements in hobby publications such as *Coins* magazine. Some may also offer current-year sets.

HOW MUCH?

In 2012, the U.S. Mint's prices on its various current-year proof and uncirculated sets ranged from $5.95 to $149.95. On the secondary market, proof sets dating back to 1956 generally range from $5 to $60. Late-date uncirculated sets generally range from $5 to $15. Some scarcer sets are higher.

COLLECTING STRATEGIES

A complete run of proof or uncirculated sets from their first issues through the current year is not a practical goal for most collectors. Thus, many focus on a few particular years or series of years.

For example, some collectors seek sets from their birth year and the birth years of their family members. They may also seek sets from other years that have significance to them.

1956 PROOF SET

1992 PROOF SET

2006-S SILVER 50 STATE QUARTERS PROOF SET

Some may also focus on sets containing a particular commemorative or other series of coins. For example, some may seek a complete collection of proof 50 State Quarters.

MINTMARKS

Proof coins from 1936 through 1964 were struck at the Philadelphia Mint and do not have mintmarks. The San Francisco Mint has produced proof coins for annual sets since 1968, and they are designated with an "S" mintmark.

Proof modern commemoratives have been struck at all four mints (Philadelphia, Denver, San Francisco, and West Point, New York) and may have a "P", "D", "S", or "W" mintmark, depending on the individual issue.

1992-W PROOF OLYMPIC GOLD $5

Annual uncirculated sets have traditionally contained an example of each coin produced for circulation at each mint in the year of issue. So if quarters were produced at Philadelphia and Denver that year, the uncirculated set would include an example of a Philadelphia-produced quarter (either no mintmark or a "P") and a Denver quarter ("D").

CONDITION

As noted, proof and uncirculated sets are specially handled and packaged at the mints. Thus, grading is less of a factor in purchasing and collecting them in original Mint packaging.

2003-P PROOF FIRST FLIGHT CENTENNIAL SILVER DOLLAR

Still, check each coin in the set before you purchase it or after you receive it in the mail. Make sure the coins' surfaces are clean and free of scratches or other significant blemishes.

The U.S. Mint has a 30-day return policy for sets purchased directly from it. Mail-order dealers, such as those who advertise in *Coins* magazine, also offer return policies. Check individual ads for specific terms.

HOW TO STORE THEM

As noted, proof and uncirculated sets are sold by the U.S. Mint in sealed, inert holders and should be left in those holders for long-term storage. Uncirculated sets from 1947 through 1958 were mounted in cardboard holders, which caused the coins to tarnish. Sets from those years will probably be found in some type of more secure aftermarket holder when offered on the secondary market.

PROOF AND UNCIRCULATED SET SPECS

The individual coins in proof and mint sets are struck to the same specifications as their circulating counterparts or, in the case of precious-metals coins, in the traditional specifications for a particular denomination in a particular metal.

CHAPTER 14

COLLECTING WORLD COINS

1780 8 REALES OF SPAIN

World coins – the hobby's common reference for coins encompassing all countries – offer a world of opportunities for collectors of all means and interests. Some historic issues dating back to the 1600s are affordable for many collectors, and like the United States, many countries today issue commemorative coins that can be purchased directly from the mint or an authorized U.S. agent.

But where do you start when the whole world of coinage is available to you?

1972 50 FRANCS OF NEW CALEDONIA

BUY A BOOK

Any collector needs to know what's available and how much it costs so he or she has a road map to their collecting pursuits. So start by buying a reference book on world coins.

An inexpensive book, such as *Warman's Coins and Paper Money*, published by Krause Publications (www.krausebooks.com), can provide a good overview of world coinage.

1903 25 CENTS OF CANADA

For a complete listing of coins available from a particular country, consult the venerable and massive *Standard Catalog of World Coins*, also from Krause Publications. The multivolume series, broken down by century, lists every coin produced in the world for the years covered. It is also available on DVD.

A subscription to the monthly *World Coin News* (www.worldcoinnews.net) provides current information on new issues from world mints and articles on world coins of all eras.

STANDARD CATALOG OF WORLD COINS

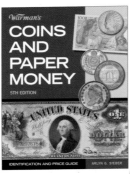

WARMAN'S COINS AND PAPER MONEY

WORLD COIN NEWS

COLLECTING STRATEGIES

When deciding which world coins to pursue, a collector should start with the basic guideline that applies to any coin-collecting pursuit: Collect what you like. A world-coin collection can be anything an individual collector wants it to be, but following are some common collecting strategies for world coins:

► BY SERIES

The traditional coin-collecting pursuit of acquiring one example of each date and mintmark within a particular series may seem daunting at first considering the vast scope of world coins. Some series within those denominations span several decades or even a century or more.

But consulting a reference, such as the *Standard Catalog of World Coins*, will reveal some shorter, affordable series that may interest an individual collector.

► BY COUNTRY

Collectors sometimes focus on coins of a particular country because of some emotional nexus with the land. It may have been their ancestors' homeland, or they may simply like the coin designs and history of a particular country.

Many strategies can be pursued within the scope of collecting by country. A collector may attempt to acquire one example of each ruler whose image appeared on the country's coinage or focus on the coinage of one particular ruler. Or

1964 5 FRANCS OF COMOROS

A WEALTH OF MINTS

Mexico's first republic, established in 1823, used 14 different mints to strike coins. All the mints used the same basic designs, but many variations exist depending on the mint.

the collector may pursue one example of each denomination or design type produced.

Any of the collecting goals could also be narrowed to a certain period – a particular century, for example, or range of years with some historical or personal significance.

1848 1 GULDEN OF THE NETHERLANDS

▶ BY REGION

A world-coin collection could also focus on a particular continent or geographic region within that continent. Examples of the former include coins of South America or the Middle East. Examples of the latter include coins of the German States, the Iberian Peninsula, or colonies of a particular country.

Assembling a complete collection of all coins of a particular region is not practical for most collectors, so a further breakdown in collecting goals are in order. That could include focusing on a particular ruler, period, denomination, or some combination thereof. It could also include some form of type collecting – one coin of each ruler, for example.

2003 10 EUROS OF THE IRISH REPUBLIC

▶ BY EMPIRE

A coin collection can be a virtual history book of an empire. It would document the dates of the empire's rise to power and fall or contraction of power. It would document the rulers that reigned over the empire. And it would document the various lands that fell under the empire's domain, including the dates of conquest and the dates of loss or independence.

1976 5 MARKS OF THE GERMAN FEDERAL REPUBLIC

▶ BY ERA

Some collectors focus on world coins of a particular era. It could be a certain century, the reign of a certain monarch, an era with personal significance to a collector, or an important historical time.

There are many other possibilities limited only to a collector's imagination and his or her historical interests.

1937 CROWN OF AUSTRALIA

▶ ONE PER COUNTRY

Another common collecting strategy is to acquire one example of the coinage of as many countries as possible. Narrowing the focus here could include a particular geographic region, century, or era.

▶ BY THEME

Modern commemorative and circulation coinage designs gave rise to collecting coins with a common theme. Examples include

2001 500 KORUN OF SLOVAKIA

COINS AS AWARDS

Russian gold ducats struck prior to Peter I (1689-1725) are believed to have been awards for military personnel rather than coinage intended for circulation. The higher the rank of the person receiving the award, the bigger the coin.

1711 HALF CROWN
OF GREAT BRITAIN

1996 1 DALASI
OF GAMBIA

coins that depict animals or ships, coins from one or more countries that commemorate a certain event, or coins of a certain date, such as 2000.

Modern coinage can complement a collection of the classics. For example, a collection of coins from the era of exploration could be accessorized by modern coins that commemorate anniversaries associated with those explorations.

A collection can also be built around a certain event. For example, Great Britain and many lands still associated with the British monarchy issued commemorative coins to mark the golden jubilee of Queen Elizabeth II's reign in 2002. These recent coins could be combined with coins from the 1950s that first depicted the queen.

▶ BY COLLECTORS CHOICE

As noted above, various aspects of the listed strategies overlap

THE CHINESE COINAGE CRISES

China nearly ceased the striking of coins in the 1930s and '40s because of war and uncontrollable inflation. The land relied on large amounts of paper currency issued by nationalist, communist, and Japanese occupation authorities.

and can be combined and mixed to form a goal that interests an individual collector. The result should be a world-coin collection that is affordable and attainable for the collector, and a collection that brings enjoyment and satisfaction.

WHERE TO GET THEM

A collector in the United States can't walk into his or her local bank and ask for a roll of Russian rubles they can search through, so world coins have to be purchased. They are, however, widely available at shows and shops, and through advertisements in hobby publications, such as *World Coin News.*

A bin full of inexpensive late-date world coins in 2-by-2 holders is a common site at shows and shops. Collectors can dig through the bins and look for coins that fit their collecting goals – be it a design theme or a certain country or a certain ruler.

Like the U.S. Mint, many world mints have Web sites through which collectors can order current-year sets and commemoratives. Reports of new issues in *World Coin News* include ordering information. Many U.S. dealers also stock current and recent world commemoratives at their shops or shows they attend.

Many world mints also display and sell their current offerings at the annual conventions and shows of the American Numismatic Association (www.money.org).

HOW MUCH?

World coins cover the gamut of numismatic values. The late-date coins in bins at shows and shops can often be purchased for less than a dollar each.

Even some coins dating back to the 1600s can be purchased for less than $20 each, depending on the coin, its composition, and its condition. A little bit of research should reveal a world-coin collecting goal that matches any collecting budget.

2002 20 KRONER OF NORWAY

MINTMARKS

Just like U.S. coins, many world coins have mintmarks indicating where they were struck. References such as the *Standard Catalog of World Coins* list the mints for each country and the marks they used to designate their coinage.

CONDITION

There is no comprehensive grading guide to world coins because of the wide range of designs among the many countries. Collectors focusing on a particular world coinage type should study examples in various condition and learn to make their own assessments of high points for wear. World-coin books usually contain some general guidelines on grading.

Fortunately, though, condition is not a critical factor for inexpensive world coins. Grading becomes more important as collectors move up in price.

HOW TO STORE THEM

Inexpensive world coins can be left in the 2-by-2 holders in which they will probably be purchased or transferred to a folder or album. But as collectors move up in price range, appropriate care should be used when handling and storing world coins, as outlined in Chapter 1.

PART 3

WHAT TO WATCH FOR

Scarce coins to know
and look for in circulation

CHAPTER 15

ON THE WATCH FOR 'WHEAT CENTS'

1911-D LINCOLN CENT

"**W**heat cents" – the common reference for Lincoln cents produced from 1909 through 1958 with the wheat-ears reverse – still turn up in circulation. The Lincoln cent rolls referenced in Chapter 2 yielded one example – a 1951-D.

Wheat cents produced from 1934 through 1958 are not valuable in typical circulated condition. Still, wheat cents are easy to spot in circulation or when searching a bulk quantity of coins, and it's still possible a scarcer, earlier date could turn up. So it's always worthwhile to check the date and mintmark on a wheat cent when one is found.

Also, a single example – such as the 1951-D mentioned above – can start a collection of wheat cents. Bulk quantities of wheat cents – ranging from a small plastic bag full of them

1951-D LINCOLN CENT

to larger cloth bags containing thousands of coins – can be purchased from dealers at shops and shows or through advertisements in hobby publications such as *Coins* magazine.

A search of these bulk quantities can speed the collection of common dates in circulated grades and could possibly yield a more valuable key date.

WHAT TO WATCH FOR

The distinctive reverse for wheat cents – two stalks of wheat surrounding the words "One Cent" – easily stands out from cents with the Lincoln Memorial reverse or the new Union Shield reverse. Following are some key dates to watch for when happening upon a wheat cent or when searching bulk quantities of the coin.

Values listed below are approximate retail values (what you could expect to pay for the coin if you were to purchase it from a dealer) for grade VF-20. The values are based on those listed in the book *U.S. Coin Digest.*

The book describes a VF-20 wheat cent as follows: "Hair, cheek, jaw, and bow-tie details will be worn but clearly separated, and wheat stalks on the reverse will be full with no weak spots."

1909-S V.D.B. LINCOLN CENT

1909-S V.D.B., $1,175

When the Lincoln cent was first issued in 1909, designer Victor David Brenner placed his initials at the bottom of the reverse between the stems of the two ears of wheat. Some, though, thought the initials were too prominent and pretentious, so they were removed after 1909 production had already begun. (They were resumed in 1918 but this time on the obverse and in a less-prominent style.)

The San Francisco Mint struck only 484,000 1909 Lincoln cents with its "S" mintmark on the obverse below the date and the designer's initials ("V.D.B.") on the reverse. Thus, this scarce variety is the king of Lincoln cents.

The coin must have both key elements – the "S" mintmark on the obverse and the "V.D.B." initials on the reverse – to command the value listed above. Other 1909 varieties are not as valuable.

The Philadelphia Mint also struck 1909 cents with the "V.D.B." initials on the reverse and no mintmark on the obverse, but mintage of this variety was almost 28 million. Value in VF-20 is about $10 to $15.

Later in 1909, Philadelphia struck more than 72 million 1909 Lincoln cents without the designer's initials on the reverse. Value in VF-20 is about $5.

Later in 1909, the San Francisco Mint struck more than 1.8 million Lincoln cents with its "S" mintmark but no designer initials. This variety is not as valuable as the 1909-S with the designer initials, but the 1909-S without the initials still commands about $165 in VF-20.

1914-D CENT

1914-D, $450

The Denver Mint produced just under 1.2 million Lincoln cents in 1914, compared with more than 75 million from the Philadelphia Mint that year. The Denver strikes have a "D" mintmark below the date on the obverse.

1922 NO MINTMARK, $1,175

All 1922 Lincoln cents were struck at the Denver Mint and are supposed to have a "D" mintmark. The mintmark, however, does not show up on some of the coins.

As the Denver Mint produced one-cent coins in 1922, it's believed that an obverse die and reverse die were damaged when they clashed in the coining press without a blank planchet in between. The reverse die was replaced, but the obverse die was repaired and put back in service. In the course of the repair, however, the mintmark apparently was removed.

1922 NO-MINTMARK CENT

The above scenario was the conclusion of a 1982 study by the American Numismatic Association Certification Service.

To command the value listed above, "plain" 1922 cents must have no trace of the mintmark and a strong reverse strike indicative of the new reverse die. Plain 1922 cents with a weak reverse strike are worth much less. Coins struck with other die combinations – some of which show traces of the "D" mintmark – are not as valuable either. Also, some 1922 cents originally struck with a "D" mintmark have been altered in an attempt to replicate the more valuable variety.

If you find a plain 1922 cent and believe it could be the valuable variety, handle the coin carefully and place it in a 2-by-2 holder. Then show it to several dealers at a show or take it to several coin shops to get some professional opinions on its authenticity.

Also note that Lincoln wheat cents struck at the Philadelphia Mint are not supposed to have mintmarks. So Lincoln cents dated other than 1922 without mintmarks are not error coins and are not exceptionally valuable. In fact, the Philadelphia Mint struck most Lincoln wheat cents in the years it produced the coin, so the Philadelphia strikes are less valuable than the San Francisco and Denver strikes of the same year.

SPECS

LINCOLN WHEAT-CENT SPECS

Designer: Victor David Brenner.

Size: 19 millimeters.

Weight: 3.11 grams.

Composition (1909-1942): 95-percent copper, 5-percent tin and zinc.

Composition (1943): Steel coated with zinc.

Composition (1944-1958): 95-percent copper, 5-percent zinc.

1931-S CENT

1931-S, $125

The San Francisco Mint struck only 866,000 Lincoln cents in 1931, compared with almost 19.4 million at the Philadelphia Mint and 4.48 million at the Denver Mint that year. To get the value listed above, the coin must be dated 1931 and must have the "S" mintmark below the date.

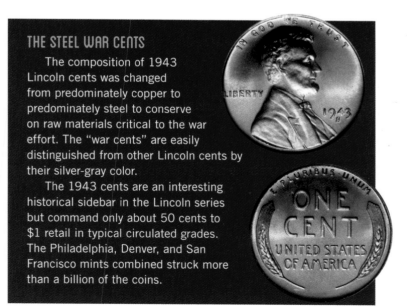

THE STEEL WAR CENTS

The composition of 1943 Lincoln cents was changed from predominately copper to predominately steel to conserve on raw materials critical to the war effort. The "war cents" are easily distinguished from other Lincoln cents by their silver-gray color.

The 1943 cents are an interesting historical sidebar in the Lincoln series but command only about 50 cents to $1 retail in typical circulated grades. The Philadelphia, Denver, and San Francisco mints combined struck more than a billion of the coins.

COIN DROPS

You say nobody will ever find a 1909-S "V.D.B." Lincoln cent in circulation again? Indeed, chances are slim that an example of this scarce variety will slip through undetected all these years, but ...

Beginning in 1990 in Seattle and continuing for several years after in a number of other cities, representatives of the weekly *Numismatic News* spent several 1909-S "V.D.B." Lincoln cents as partial payment for such sundry items as lunch or ice cream. The "coin drops," as they came to be known, were publicity stunts for coin collecting in advance of American Numismatic Association conventions held in the respective cities in various years.

News releases announcing the drops were sent to local media, and they generated prominent newspaper and television news coverage for the hobby and upcoming convention.

None of the coins was ever reported found, so just maybe, somewhere out there ...

CHAPTER 16

ON THE WATCH FOR DOUBLED-DIE LINCOLN CENTS

I f you see double on a Lincoln cent, you could be seeing hundreds of dollars in profit. Coins that show a distinctive doubling of their design features – like the coin is out of focus – are valued by collectors. Some doubled-die coins are common and worth only a few dollars each; others command higher prices.

Following are five doubled-die Lincoln cents that have been identified by experts and are commonly listed in coin value guides. Circulating cents dated 1955, 1972, 1983, 1984, and 1995 should be checked for this doubling.

Values listed below are approximate retail values (the price you could expect to pay if purchasing the coin from a dealer) and are based on the value listings in the book *U.S. Coin Digest.*

THE STORY BEHIND THE COINS

To understand doubled-die coins, one must first understand how coins are produced. Following are the three major steps in the manufacturing process:

1. BLANKS ARE PRODUCED.

A "blank" is a round, flat piece of coin metal punched from a sheet or strip of metal. It's then given a raised edge, or rim, and it becomes a "planchet."

BIN OF PLANCHETS

The planchet is the same size and composition of the coin it will become, but at this point, it is just a blank piece of metal with no design.

2. DIES ARE PRODUCED.

A die is a round piece of hard metal with a mirror image of the coin design engraved in recess on its face. It takes two dies to produce a coin – one with the obverse design on it and one with the reverse design on it.

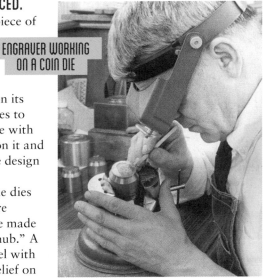

ENGRAVER WORKING ON A COIN DIE

Working dies – the dies from which coins are actually struck – are made by a tool called a "hub." A hub is a piece of steel with the coin design in relief on it – the same as the relief design (with the design features raised above the coin's surface) on a coin.

A blank die is softened by heating it, and then the hub is forced into the die face, which forms the incuse, mirror image of the coin design on the die face. Thousands of working dies can be made from a single hub.

3. COINS ARE STRUCK.

To produce the actual coin, a blank is fed into a coining press between the obverse die and reverse die. The two dies are pressed onto the blank at tremendous pressure – about 30 tons per square inch to produce a one-cent coin – impressing the design image onto the blank. The finished coin is then ejected from the press and into a hopper.

All of this happen in a fraction of a second. Modern coin presses are capable of producing hundreds of coins a minute.

ROW OF COIN PRESSES

HOW DOUBLING OCCURS

To produce a working die, it must receive multiple impressions, or pressings, from the hub. Between impressions, the die is removed from the die press and softened again.

If the hub and die are not lined up properly when placed back on the die press, the subsequent pressings from the hub will not line up with the existing impression on the working die made by previous pressings. The result is a doubling of the design features on the die because the subsequent pressing is slightly offset from the previous ones.

Because the design is now doubled on the die, all coins struck from the die will show the doubling on either their obverse or reverse, depending on which die was affected by the doubling.

Because the hubbing process is the source of the doubling, this type of doubling is referred to by collectors as "hub doubling." "Most forms of hub doubling show as well-rounded, overlapping images in relief, with distinct separation lines between those images," say authors Brian Allen and Ken Potter in their book *Strike It Rich With Pocket Change* (Krause Publications, 2006).

WHAT TO WATCH FOR

▶ 1955 DOUBLED-DIE LINCOLN CENT, $2,350 IN GRADE XF-40

This is the king of doubled-die Lincoln cents, partly because it's the oldest and partly because the doubling is so distinct. It can be clearly seen in the date.

The doubling occurs only on the 1955 Philadelphia strikes, which do not have a mintmark. It does not occur on the 1955 Lincoln cents with a "D" mintmark for Denver or an "S" mintmark for San Francisco.

1955 DOUBLED-DIE CENT DETAIL

DOUBLED WITH TWO DS

Some sources refer to "double-die" coins, but the term is more precisely written as "doubled-die" because the design on the working die is doubled, creating the doubled image on the coin. The doubled image did not occur because "double dies" were used.

▶ 1972 DOUBLED-DIE LINCOLN CENT, $285 IN GRADE XF-40

There are several known doubled-die 1972 Lincoln cents from all three mints, but the most valuable are Philadelphia strikes with distinctive doubling on the obverse. It can be seen in the date, the word "Liberty," and the motto "In God We Trust."

▶ 1983 DOUBLED-DIE LINCOLN CENT, $400 IN GRADE MS-65

The doubling occurs on the reverse and is not quite as distinctive as the 1955 and 1972 cents. Check the lettering on the reverse, particularly in the words "One Cent." The doubling again occurs only on Philadelphia coins (those without mintmarks).

1983 DOUBLED-DIE CENT

▶ 1984 DOUBLED-DIE LINCOLN CENT, $275 IN GRADE MS-65

The doubling again occurs on the obverse and again is more subtle than earlier doubled-die cents. Check around Lincoln's ear lobe for a doubled image. This doubling occurs only on 1984 Lincoln cents struck at Philadelphia.

1984 DOUBLED-DIE LINCOLN CENT

▶ 1995 DOUBLED-DIE LINCOLN CENT, $20 IN GRADE XF-40

The doubling occurs on the obverse and can be best seen in the letters "ber" in the word "Liberty." It can also be seen in the motto "In God We Trust." This doubling occurs only on 1995 Lincoln cents struck at Philadelphia.

1995 DOUBLED-DIE LINCOLN CENT DETAIL

WHAT TO DO IF YOU FIND ONE

If you believe you've found one of the doubled-die Lincoln cents listed above, particularly one of the more valuable dates, handle the coin carefully and place it in a 2-by-2 holder. Then show it to several dealers at a show or take it to several coin shops to get some professional opinions on its authenticity.

THE END OF HUB DOUBLING?

Have we seen the last of doubled-die coins? Maybe. In the 1990s, the U.S. Mint switched to a more modern "single-squeeze" process for producing working coin dies from a hub rather than the old multiple-impression process. The new process has "virtually eliminated the possibility of hub doubling on coins in the United States starting in 1997 for the cent and five-cent coins and the balance of denominations in 1998," say authors Brian Allen and Ken Potter in their book *Strike It Rich With Pocket Change*.

MAKE YOUR OWN COIN DIE (SORT OF)

Here's another way to see how coin dies work:

1. Find a newer quarter with nice, sharp detail in its design. (Make sure it's a coin that you don't want to save for your collection.)
2. Place a small piece of aluminum foil over it.
3. Press the foil lightly over the coin and hold it so it won't slip.
4. Take the eraser end of a pencil and rub the eraser over the foil. Watch how the coin's design starts to show through the foil.
5. When the whole design shows through the foil, carefully lift the foil off the coin.
6. Look at the other side of the foil – the inside part that was pressed against the coin. See how the design appears backward on the inside part of the foil? Notice, too, how the raised parts of the design on the coin, such as lettering, look indented on the foil.

That's how the design looks on a coin die. If you could take your aluminum foil "die" and press it hard enough into some soft surface, the design would come out forward-facing on the surface, similar to a coin die pressing into a planchet on a coining press.

ALUMINUM-FOIL
COIN DIE

CHAPTER 17

ON THE WATCH FOR 1950-D JEFFERSON NICKELS

1950-D JEFFERSON NICKEL REVERSE

In the 1950s and '60s, the 1950-D Jefferson nickel was one of the hottest things on the market. Demand for this otherwise unassuming coin has cooled off in recent years, but it's still worth putting aside if you happen upon one when searching rolls of Jefferson nickels.

THE STORY BEHIND THE COIN

Coin collecting was entering a boom period in the early 1950s. War veterans came home and started earning a living wage, which allowed them to pursue hobbies like coin collecting. Older collectible coins, such as Indian cents and Liberty nickels, could still be found in circulation.

There were more publications on coin collecting, so there was more information on the hobby. Collectors became more aware of hobby news like mintage figures for current or late-date coinage.

Thus, when it became known in the early 1950s that the Denver Mint produced "only" 2.63 million 5-cent coins in 1950, the rush was one for 1950-D Jefferson nickels. In contrast, the Philadelphia Mint produced more than 9.8 million nickels that year.

In 1949, Philadelphia produced more than 60 million nickels, Denver produced more than 36 million, and San Francisco produced more than 9.7 million. In 1951, Philadelphia produced more than 28 million nickels, Denver produced more than 20 million, and San Francisco produced more than 7.7 million.

Although a couple of million coins is still a couple of million coins, the 1950-D mintage was significantly lower than other Jefferson nickel date and mintmark combinations of the era. In 1957, Denver produced more than 168 million Jefferson nickels.

Collectors of the 1950s began hoarding every 1950-D Jefferson nickel they could get their hands on. By 1964, when the Philadelphia and Denver mints combined produced more than 2.8 billion Jefferson nickels, the 1950-D's mintage seemed even more paltry.

Still, though, a couple of million coins is a couple of million coins. With collectors putting aside every '50-D nickel they could find, it became apparent later in the 1960s and '70s that plenty of collectible examples

1950-D JEFFERSON NICKEL OBVERSE

existed to meet market demand.

Values for 1950-D nickels have stabilized since the late 1950s and early '60s, but they still have the lowest mintage in the Jefferson series. With nickel mintages today in the hundreds of millions, it's highly unlikely the U.S. Mint will ever produce a circulating Jefferson nickel with a lower mintage.

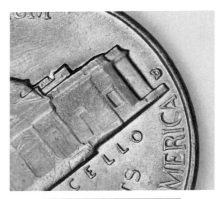

1950-D JEFFERSON NICKEL MINTMARK DETAIL

WHAT TO WATCH FOR

They're easy to spot. Look for the 1950 date on the obverse and the "D" mintmark on the reverse to the right of Monticello.

HOW MUCH?

Retail values for 1950-D Jefferson nickels in typical circulated grades range from $10 to $15. Even well-worn examples reach the lower level of that price range.

WHAT TO DO IF YOU FIND ONE

Follow the rules in Chapter 1 for safe handling of coins and place the coin in a 2-by-2 holder or another type of safe storage system in which both sides of the coin are protected.

THE DENVER MINT

An 1862 congressional act established a U.S. assay office in Denver, but full-fledged branch-mint status came later. Coin production began in 1906. Denver continues to produce all denominations of currently circulating coins.

In U.S. coinage history, Denver shares its "D" mintmark with the Dahlonega (Georgia) Mint, which struck gold coins in various years from 1838 through 1861.

CHAPTER 18

ON THE WATCH FOR 1982 NO-MINTMARK DIMES

1982 NO-MINTMARK DIME

Oops.

That may have been the collective reaction of U.S. Mint officials and workers when they discovered an important design element was left off a Philadelphia Mint working die for 1982 dimes – namely, the "P" mintmark.

In the years since its discovery, the 1982 no-mintmark dime has become one of the classic error coins of all time. It's believed the number struck was small, but it's still a candidate to turn up in circulation for those who know of its existence and what to look for.

THE STORY BEHIND THE COIN

The Roosevelt dime was introduced in 1946 as a tribute to the late President Franklin D. Roosevelt. Calls for Roosevelt to be honored on a coin came soon after his death on April 12, 1945.

Congressional approval is required to change any coin design that has been used for less than 25 years. At the time of Roosevelt's death, the Lincoln cent (introduced in 1909), the so-called Mercury dime (1916), and the Walking Liberty half dollar (1916) were eligible for redesign.

The dime was chosen for Roosevelt because the March of Dimes was a fund-raising campaign for the National Foundation for Infantile Paralysis, which Roosevelt established in 1938. Roosevelt suffered from the disease, commonly called polio. The NFIP later adapted March of Dimes as its official name, and the organization today focuses on prenatal and newborn health issues.

1942 MERCURY DIME

Mint engraver John R. Sinnock designed the Roosevelt dime. The Philadelphia, Denver, and San Francisco mints produced circulation strikes of the Roosevelt dime from 1946 through 1955. Denver and Philadelphia have continued to produce Roosevelt dimes for circulation since 1956. San Francisco has produced proof versions since 1968.

From 1946 through 1964, Roosevelt dimes produced at Philadelphia did not have a mintmark. Those produced at Denver had a "D" mintmark, and those produced at San Francisco had an "S" mintmark.

From 1965 through 1967, no U.S. coins had mintmarks.

1968 ROOSEVELT DIME

From 1968 through 1979, Roosevelt dimes produced at Philadelphia did not have a mintmark, but those produced at Denver resumed the "D" mintmark and the proof versions produced at San Francisco carried an "S" mintmark.

Beginning in 1980, the "P" mintmark was added to Roosevelt dimes produced at Philadelphia. Whatever the reason, a working die without a "P" mintmark added to it was put into production at Philadelphia and apparently went unnoticed for a significant period.

The error became known to the coin-collecting community in early 1983 when 1982 dimes without mintmarks started showing up in Ohio.

WHY NO MINTMARKS IN 1965-1967?

Mintmarks were eliminated from U.S. coins dated 1965-1967 in an effort to streamline production. It was one of several steps the U.S. Mint took at the time in response to a coin shortage.

See Chapter 20 for more on the coin shortage of the early to mid-1960s.

WHAT TO WATCH FOR

The error appears on Roosevelt dimes dated 1982 only. The mintmark is supposed to appear on the obverse just above the date. This area should show absolutely no trace of a mintmark.

1982 NO MINTMARK DIME

1971-D ROOSEVELT DIME

A faint outline of a mintmark in this area may indicate simply a weak strike, possibly caused by dirt or grease filling in the mintmark area on the working die, or a weak attempt at altering a 1982 dime with a mintmark.

HOW MUCH?

A 1982 no-mintmark dime is worth about $25 to $50 in typical circulated grades.

WHAT TO DO IF YOU FIND ONE

If you believe you've found a 1982 no-mintmark dime, follow the rules in Chapter 1 for safe handling of coins and place it in a 2-by-2 holder. Then show it to several dealers at a show or take it to several coin shops to get some professional opinions on its authenticity.

IT'S ONLY THE '82 THAT'S VALUABLE

"Hey, I found a 1978 dime without a mintmark. How much is it worth?"

Answer: 10 cents.

As noted, Roosevelt dimes produced at Philadelphia before 1980 are not supposed to have mintmarks. Therefore, pre-1980 Roosevelt dimes produced for circulation without mintmarks are not errors and are not scarce.

It is only the 1982-dated dime without a mintmark that is in error.

CHAPTER 19

ON THE WATCH FOR THE EXTRA-LEAF WISCONSIN QUARTER

2004-D WISCONSIN QUARTER

It's one of those things that only a sharp-eyed coin collector would notice, but it set the coin-collecting community on its collective ear, so to speak, when it was discovered.

In early 2005, a number of 2004 Wisconsin quarters, part of the U.S. Mint's 50 State Quarters program, were discovered with what appears to be an extra leaf in the ear of corn on the reverse. The coin community and even the general media – including CNN, *USA Today*, and National Public Radio – were abuzz with the news, and values for the variety shot up.

Values have since settled in, but the two varieties of extra-leaf Wisconsin quarters are still some of the most significant coins that can conceivably be found in circulation.

THE STORY BEHIND THE COIN

The Wisconsin quarter was released October 25, 2004, with the usual amount of fanfare accompanying the release of each coin in the 50 State Quarters program within each respective state. The reverse features simplistic depictions of a cow, an ear of corn, and a wheel of cheese – certainly symbolic of one major industry in the state but falling short on artistic merit.

In early 2005, however, the coin started making national news when collectors in the Southwest noticed the ear of corn appeared to have an extra leaf on some coins produced at the Denver Mint ("D" mintmark). When the news broke, the scramble was on to find the coins with the unintentional variety, and speculation as to what caused it was rampant.

The extra leaf appears to the viewer's left of the ear of corn beneath the large turned-down leaf. As the coins surfaced, two varieties were detected: One has the extra leaf pointed downward (listed as "leaf low" in some value guides), and the second has the extra leaf pointed upward ("leaf high").

About a year after the coins were discovered, the mystery as to what caused the variety was solved when *USA Today* obtained a copy of the Mint's official report on the incident through the Freedom of Information Act. In its January 20, 2006, issue, the newspaper reported that an ill-timed meal break by a Denver Mint worker was the cause.

The report said a press operator at the branch mint noticed blemishes on the Wisconsin quarters being produced on one of the

CHEESE WHIZ! THAT'S A LOT OF IDEAS

According to the U.S. Mint's official profile of the Wisconsin state quarter, the state's governor received more than 9,600 design suggestions for the coin. That's more than half the number of dairy farms in the state (17,000) and almost 30 times the number of varieties of cheeses produced in the state (more than 350).

five machines he was operating. He stopped the machine, but then left for a meal break before correcting the problem.

When he returned to work, the machine was running again, so he assumed that another worker had changed the working die being used to strike the quarters. About an hour and a half later, it was discovered the problem had not been resolved and that thousands of coins with the extra leaf had been struck and comingled with regular coins produced by other presses.

By the time the mistake was discovered, according to the *USA Today* report, the coins were already bagged and ready for shipment. The newspaper reported that as many as 50,000 entered circulation. The book *U.S. Coin Digest* estimates the total mintage at 12,000.

WHAT TO WATCH FOR

The variety appears on 2004 Wisconsin quarters struck at the Denver Mint only ("D" mintmark on the obverse below the words "In God We Trust"). Check the area to the left of the ear of corn, below the large turned-down leaf on the reverse, for another smaller leaf emanating from the ear.

NORMAL WISCONSIN QUARTER DETAIL

On some coins with the variety, the extra leaf is turned down in an arc toward the wheel of cheese ("leaf low"). On others, it points upward toward the larger leaf above it ("leaf high").

"LEAF LOW" WISCONSIN QUARTER DETAIL

"LEAF HIGH" WISCONSIN QUARTER DETAIL

HOW MUCH?

The "leaf high" variety is the scarcer of the two, according to *U.S. Coin Digest*. The book estimates its mintage at 3,000. Mintage for the "leaf low" variety is estimated at 9,000.

Three-coin sets (one regular example and the two varieties) in high uncirculated grades have sold for thousands of dollars each. Expect much less for one found in circulation with typical wear – around $50. The scarcer "leaf high" variety will garner a bit more.

WHAT TO DO IF YOU FIND ONE

Follow the rules in Chapter 1 for safe handling of coins and place the coin in a 2-by-2 holder or another type of safe storage system in which both sides of the coin are protected. Then show it to several dealers at a show or take it to several coin shops to get some professional opinions on its authenticity. As always, scarce varieties are susceptible to nefarious attempts at replication by altering a common coin.

CHAPTER 20

ON THE WATCH FOR SILVER COINS

1964 ROOSEVELT DIME

Until 1965, U.S. dimes, quarters, and half dollars were struck in the traditional composition of 90-percent silver and 10-percent copper. In early 2013, silver bullion traded at about $30 a troy ounce. That made the silver in a pre-1965 quarter worth about $5.40.

Although most of the old silver coinage has been culled from circulation over the years, silver coins of current design (Roosevelt dime, Washington quarter, and Kennedy half dollar) still slip through now and then.

THE STORY BEHIND THE COINS

Until 1961, the U.S. government controlled the price of silver in the country, setting it at 92.5 cents a troy ounce. But after 1961, silver bullion was allowed to trade on the free market and government controls on its price were lifted.

Silver soon shot up to $1.29 an ounce.

HOW MUCH SILVER?

Following are actual silver weights for pre-1965 dimes, quarters, and half dollars:

Dime: 0.0723 troy ounces.
Quarter: 0.1808 troy ounces.
Half dollar: 0.3617 troy ounces.

By 1964, it cost the government more than 25 cents to produce a quarter because of the increase in silver prices. The high cost of silver coupled with increasing demand for coinage, in part from

1953 WASHINGTON QUARTER

1966 WASHINGTON QUARTER

the growing popularity of vending machines, led to a coin shortage in the country.

In response, President Lyndon Johnson signed into law the Coinage Act of 1965, which eliminated silver from the dime and quarter, and replaced it with a clad composition consisting largely of copper. The half dollar was reduced to 40-percent silver (see Chapter 21).

The act also suspended the production of proof and uncirculated sets for sale to collectors so the U.S. Mint could concentrate on circulating-coin production. It also eliminated mintmarks on coins in another effort to streamline production.

Any silver coins still produced in 1965 were to be dated 1964; the new clad coins were to be dated 1965 until the shortage was resolved, even if that was into 1966 or beyond.

The clad coins continue to be struck today, although the U.S. Mint started to experiment with even cheaper coinage metals in response to rising prices for copper. As the clad coins entered circulation, the public hoarded the old silver coins, which were worth more than face value because of their precious-metal content and the rising price of silver.

KEY QUARTER DATES

Washington quarters with "D" and "S" mintmarks dated from the series inception in 1932 through 1940 command numismatic premiums above their bullion value. The 1932-D and 1932-S are the two key dates and command significant premiums – about $200 each in typical circulated grades.

There are also two over-engraved mintmarks to watch for: the 1950 "D" over "S" and the 1950 "S" over "D". In these two instances, the dominant mintmark was engraved over the underlying mintmark on the working die. On the resulting coins, a faint outline of the underlying mintmark can be seen under the dominant mintmark.

Each variety is worth about $100 in typical circulated grades. The mintmark for these dates appears on the reverse above the "R" in the word "Quarter."

WHAT TO WATCH FOR

The silver dimes, quarters, and half dollars are easy to distinguish: Any example dated 1964 or earlier has a composition consisting of 90-percent silver. In addition, it's always a good idea to check found coins for key dates – those with lower mintages that command a numismatic premium over their bullion value. To determine key dates, consult a current value guide, such as *U.S. Coin Digest*.

HOW MUCH?

The accompanying silver value chart shows the bullion value of silver dimes, quarters, and half dollars at various silver prices. Many Web sites report current silver prices, including the financial sections of daily newspapers.

SILVER VALUE CHART

The following chart shows the precious-metal value of silver dimes, quarters, and half dollars at various prices per troy ounce for silver bullion.

	15.00	17.50	20.00	22.50	25.00	30.00	35.00
Dime	1.08	1.26	1.44	1.62	1.80	2.16	2.53
Quarter	2.71	3.16	3.61	4.06	4.52	5.42	6.32
Half dollar	5.42	6.32	7.23	8.13	9.04	10.85	12.65

WHAT TO DO IF YOU FIND ONE

No special precautions need to be taken with silver coins found in circulation if they display the typical amount of wear one can expect to find on them. For a coin in better condition or a key date, follow the rules in Chapter 1 for safe handling of coins and place it in a 2-by-2 holder or another storage system in which both

1936 WASHINGTON QUARTER

1945 WASHINGTON QUARTER

sides of the coin are protected.

If you want to sell the coin, it's unlikely a dealer will want to mess around with purchasing just one silver dime or quarter unless it is a key date. The dealer may, however, be interested in purchasing a larger quantity of silver coins for their bullion value.

Consider keeping any silver coins found and using them as a start to a collection of older Roosevelt dimes, Washington quarters, or Kennedy half dollars.

WAR NICKELS

When searching Jefferson nickels, collectors should watch for examples dated 1942 through 1945. These wartime nickels were struck from 56-percent copper, 35-percent silver, and 9-percent manganese. They contain 0.0563 troy ounces of silver.

If the date isn't enough to distinguish them, look for the big mintmark ("P", "D", or "S") above the dome of Monticello on the reverse. For nickels struck during the war years, the mintmark was moved from its usual location to the right of Jefferson's home.

1943 JEFFERSON NICKEL

CHAPTER 21

ON THE WATCH FOR 1965–1970 KENNEDY HALF DOLLARS

Kennedy half dollars dated 1965 through 1970 were also the targets of hoarders in the 1960s and '70s. The reason was the 0.148 troy ounces of precious metal in each of the 40-percent-silver coins.

Many were culled from pocket change and sources of bulk change during this time, but others may still be hiding in circulation thanks to the continued use of the Kennedy design for the half dollar and a lack of knowledge among the general public about the coin's precious-metal content.

KEY DATE: 1970-D

The U.S. Mint produced only 2.15 million 1970 Kennedy half dollars for circulation, all with a "D" mintmark for Denver. According to the book *U.S. Coin Digest*, a 1970-D Kennedy half dollar sells for about $50 in the uncirculated grade of MS-65.

Prices for a coin in typical circulated grades will be substantially lower, but a 1970-D Kennedy half dollar found in circulation may still be worth a little extra care in its handling and storage.

THE STORY BEHIND THE COIN

The U.S. dime, quarter, and half dollar were still struck in the 90-percent-silver composition when the Kennedy half dollar was put on the fast track to production in late 1963 and early 1964 (see Chapter 8). So the Kennedy half saw one year (1964) of production in the traditional composition.

The Coinage Act of 1965, however, which converted the dime and quarter to a base-metal clad composition, changed the half dollar's composition to 80-percent silver and 20-percent copper bonded to a core of 20.9-percent silver and 79.1-percent copper. The net result was the 40-percent-silver composition and the 0.148 troy ounces of precious metal.

As the only precious-metal U.S. coins still in production, many 1965-1970 Kennedy half dollars were squirreled away by the public instead of remaining in circulation, even though silver prices at the time kept the half's bullion value below its 50-cent face value. The U.S. Mint couldn't produce enough of them to meet demand. It produced more than 295 million 1967 Kennedy half dollars for circulation. The following year, the Denver Mint (the only mint to produce half dollars for circulation that year) produced more than 246 million. The large mintages were also cutting into the government's silver reserves.

Congress responded in 1970 by passing a law changing the Kennedy half dollar's composition to the same clad composition used in the dime and quarter starting with 1965-dated coins (75-percent copper and 25-percent nickel bonded to a pure-copper core). The clad composition for the half dollar was first used on 1971-dated coins and continues today, although the U.S. Mint started experimenting with other coinage metals in response to rising copper prices.

The switch to a base-metal composition and increasing silver prices accelerated the culling of 1965-1970 Kennedy half dollars from circulation in the 1970s. In 1974, the average daily price of silver was $4.71, making the bullion content of a 40-percent-silver half dollar worth about 70 cents.

WHAT TO WATCH FOR

A simple date check – 1965 through 1970 – is all that's required to detect a 40-percent-silver Kennedy half dollar. Circulation strikes without mintmarks were produced from 1965 through 1967. Collector versions for inclusion in Special Mint Sets (see Chapter 13) were also struck in those years.

From 1968 through 1970, only the Denver Mint produced Kennedy half dollars for circulation. They carry a "D" mintmark on the obverse below Kennedy's neckline.

The San Francisco Mint produced only proof examples in 1968, 1969, and 1970. These special versions were sold directly to collectors and have an "S" mintmark.

WHAT TO DO IF YOU FIND ONE

No special precautions need to be taken with 40-percent-silver Kennedy half dollars found in circulation if they display the typical amount of wear one can expect to find on them. For a coin

SILVER VALUE CHART

The following chart shows the precious-metal value of 40-percent-silver Kennedy half dollars at various prices per troy ounce for silver bullion. Silver prices are on the top row; the corresponding coin bullion value is on the bottom row.

15.00	17.50	20.00	22.50	25.00	30.00	35.00
2.22	2.59	2.96	3.33	3.70	4.44	5.18

in better condition, particularly the 1970-D (see sidebar), follow the rules in Chapter 1 for safe handling of coins and place it in a 2-by-2 holder or another storage system in which both sides of the coin are protected.

SPECIAL MINT SETS

If you want to sell the coin, it's unlikely a dealer will want to bother with purchasing just one 40-percent-silver Kennedy half dollar. The dealer may, however, be interested in purchasing a larger quantity of silver coins for their bullion value.

Consider keeping any 40-percent-silver half dollars found in circulation and putting them toward a complete collection of Kennedy half dollars from 1964 to date.

40-PERCENT-SILVER
KENNEDY HALF DOLLAR CHECKLIST

_____ 1965

_____ 1965 Special Mint Set version

_____ 1966

_____ 1966 Special Mint Set version

_____ 1967

_____ 1967 Special Mint Set version

_____ 1968-D

_____ 1968-S (proof only)

_____ 1969-D

_____ 1969-S (proof only)

_____ 1970-D

_____ 1970-S (proof only)

1969-S KENNEDY HALF DOLLAR

PART 4

SPEAKING OF COINS

Numismatic terms to know
and an introduction to grading

CHAPTER 22

THE LANGUAGE OF COINS

Like any field, coin collecting has its own jargon and lingo. A study of the following terms will have you talking like a numismatist in no time.

1887-O SILVER DOLLAR

ALLOY

A metal or mixture of metals added to the primary metal in the coinage composition, often as a means of facilitating hardness during striking. For example, most U.S. silver and gold coins contain an alloy of 90-percent precious metal and 10-percent copper.

AUTHENTICATION

The act of determining whether a coin, medal, token, or other related item is a genuine product of the issuing authority. The authenticating is usually done by a recognized expert in the field, either an individual or a professional grading service.

BAG MARKS

Scrapes and impairments to a coin's surface obtained after minting by contact with other coins. The term originates from the storage of coins in bags, but such marks can occur as coins are ejected from the presses and dumped into hoppers in bulk. A larger coin is more susceptible to marks, which affect its grade and, therefore, its value.

BASE METAL

A metal with low intrinsic value. The clad coins struck for circulation in the United States today are considered base-metal coins because they are composed of copper and nickel rather than precious metals such as gold, silver, or platinum.

COIN ALIGNMENT

Take a coin out of your pocket and hold it between your thumb and forefinger with the obverse ("heads" side) facing you. Using the forefinger on your other hand, spin it around so the reverse ("tails" side) faces you. The reverse will be upside down. This alignment of obverse and reverse is called "coin alignment" because it has traditionally been used on coins. In contrast, see the entries below for "medal" and "medal alignment."

DEMONSTRATION OF COIN ALIGNMENT

2002 GREAT BRITAIN ELIZABETH II GOLDEN JUBILEE COMMEMORATIVE

COMMEMORATIVE

An official, government-issued coin to honor a special event or person. Commemoratives are usually sold directly to collectors at a premium above face value by the issuing authority, such as the U.S. Mint.

2000 ISLE OF MAN MILLENNIUM CROWN

COUNTERFEIT

A coin or medal or other numismatic item made fraudulently either for entry into circulation or sale to collectors. Among the general public, counterfeiting is usually associated with paper money that is illicitly produced and spent. In numismatics, counterfeiting can involve attempts to produce a rare coin from scratch or altering a common coin to make it look like a scarce variety. For instance, a counterfeiter may try to remove the mintmark from a 1982 Roosevelt dime to try to pass it off as one of the scarce 1982-no-mintmark dimes (see Chapter 18).

DIE

A cylindrical piece of metal containing an incused image of a coin design that imparts a raised image when stamped into a planchet on a coining press.

1903
GOLD $20

DOUBLE EAGLE
An official name, as designated by law, for the U.S. gold $20 coin
struck for circulation from 1849 through 1932.

1901
GOLD $10

EAGLE
An official name, as designated by law, for the U.S. gold $10 coin
struck for circulation from 1795 through 1933.

SMOOTH EDGE
AND REEDED EDGE

EDGE

The cylindrical surface of a coin between the two sides. The edge can be plain, reeded, ornamented, or lettered.

LETTER EDGES ON PRESIDENTIAL DOLLAR COINS

FACE VALUE

The nominal, legal-tender value assigned to a given coin by the governing authority.

GRADING

The largely subjective practice of providing a numerical or adjectival ranking of a coin's condition. See Chapter 23 for more on grading.

1899 GOLD $5

HALF EAGLE

An official name, as designated by law, for the U.S. gold $5 coin struck for circulation from 1795 through 1929.

HUB

A piece of die steel showing the coinage devices in relief, or raised, as they are on a coin. The hub is pressed into a blank die, resulting in an incused, mirror image on the die. The die is then pressed into a planchet, or coin blank, on a coining press to produce a coin.

LETTERED EDGE

Incused or raised lettering on a coin's edge.

U.S. MINT NEW FRONTIER MEDAL

MEDAL

A coinlike object produced to commemorate an event or person. Unlike a coin, a medal is not legal tender and has no value imprinted on it. It is usually larger (2 inches in diameter, for example) and thicker than a coin. Governments sometimes issue and sell medals. For example, the U.S. Mint produces and sells medals to commemorate the inauguration of a new president. Private organizations and individuals can also issue medals.

MEDAL ALIGNMENT

Medals are generally struck with the coinage dies facing the same direction during striking. If you were to conduct the same exercise described under "coin alignment" with a medal, the reverse would be right side up instead of upside down.

MINTAGE

The total number of coins struck during a given time frame, generally one year. Coin listings in value guides, such as the book *U.S. Coin Digest*.

MINTMARK

A letter or other marking on a coin's surface to identify the mint at which the coin was struck. Mintmarks currently used on U.S. coins are "P" for the Philadelphia Mint, "D" for Denver, "S" for San Francisco, and "W" for West Point.

NUMISMATICS, NUMISMATIST

Numismatics (pronounced "new-miss-MAT-iks") is the science, study, or collecting of coins, tokens, medals, paper money, and related items. One who participates in this science is a numismatist (pronounced "new-MISS-mat-ist").

PLANCHET

A blank disc of metal on which the image of the dies are impressed in a coining press, resulting in a finished coin. Also sometimes called a "blank."

GREAT BRITAIN PROOF 2000 50 PENCE

PROOF

A type of coin produced specially for sale to collectors. It is produced from specially polished dies and planchets, and receives more than one striking in the coining press. Modern silver proofs often have what are called "frosted" surfaces, which is a white finish on the raised design devices, such as a bust on the obverse.

1859 GOLD $2.50

QUARTER EAGLE

An official name, as designated by law, for the U.S. gold $2.50 coin struck for circulation from 1796 through 1929.

REEDING

The serrated (toothlike) ornamentation applied to a coin's edge during striking. U.S. dimes, quarters, and half dollars currently produced for circulation have reeded edges. The 1-cent and 5-cent coins have plain edges.

SERIES

The complete group of coins of the same denomination and design, and representing all issuing mints. For example, the Roosevelt dime series has been struck since 1946. The America the Beautiful Quarters are a coin series.

SLABS

A nickname for coins graded by a professional coin-grading service and then sealed in a plastic holder with the coin's description, the grade assigned by the service, and a unique serial number.

COIN IN A SLAB

See Chapter 23 for more on grading and grading services.

MERCHANT TOKEN

TOKEN

A privately issued piece, generally in round metal, with a represented value in trade or for a service. Businesses in the 1800s and early 1900s used tokens as promotional items and, in some cases, as substitutes for change during coinage shortages. The tokens carried inscriptions such as "Good for 10 Cents at Bob's Grocery." In more recent years, casinos have issued tokens. The tokens are sold to patrons, who use them instead of cash when gambling.

TYPE COIN

A coin that is collected because it represents a basic design of a particular denomination. For example, a type set of 20th-century U.S. quarters would consist of one example each of the Barber type (1892-1916), the Standing Liberty type (1916-1930), and the Washington type (1932 to present). Many collectors turn to type collecting because it is easier and provides more financial flexibility than trying to assemble an example of each date and mintmark combination of an entire series. In the quarter type-set example above, type collectors can choose any date and mintmark combination from any of the dates listed for each type. The collecting goal is an example of each design type rather than specific date and mintmark combinations.

VARIETY

Any coin with a design feature different from the usual design for a particular coin series. The 1982 no-mintmark dime (see Chapter 18), for example, is a variety of the Roosevelt dime. The extra-leaf Wisconsin quarters (see Chapter 19) are varieties of that series.

PARTS OF A COIN

EXERGUE

The lower segment of a coin, below the main design, generally separated by a line and often containing the date, designer initials, and mintmark.

OBVERSE

The front, or "heads," side of a coin.

RELIEF

Describes the portion of a design raised above the coin's surface, such as the bust of Washington on the quarter. The highest points of a coin's relief are most susceptible to wear in circulation and are the key areas to check when grading a coin.

FIELD

The flat area of a coin's obverse or reverse, devoid of design devices or inscriptions.

LEGEND

The coin's principal lettering, generally shown along its outer perimeter. "United States of America" is an example of a legend on U.S. coins.

REVERSE

The back, or "tails" side, of a coin.

RIM

The raised area of a coin bordering the edge and surrounding the field.

CHAPTER 23
AN INTRODUCTION TO GRADING

1882 INDIAN CENT

Classified ads for used cars often contain some indication of the vehicle's condition. "Good condition." "Clean car." "No rust." "Low mileage." "Good runner."

The condition designations are informal and open to interpretation. Ultimately, a potential buyer must look at the car, assess its condition firsthand, and determine whether he or she wants to make a viable offer for it. If the buyer and seller can't get together on a price or the buyer determines the car just isn't right for him or her, then the buyer should thank the seller for his or her time and keep looking.

Coin grading – the process of assigning designated terms to concisely describe a coin's condition – has a more formal and defined structure than the informal language often used in selling used cars. Still, it is not an exact process. Two longtime collectors can legitimately disagree on a coin's grade, especially among uncirculated coins.

1907 LIBERTY NICKEL

Like buying a used car, a coin buyer must look at the coin, assess its condition firsthand, and determine whether he or she wants to make a viable offer for it. If the buyer or seller can't get together on a price or the buyer determines the coin just isn't right for them, then the buyer should thank the seller for his or her time and keep looking.

Hobby legend says that a collector walked up to a crusty old dealer at a show one time and asked the dealer to grade a coin the collector brought with him. The dealer looked at the coin and said, "I grade it a hundred dollars."

Such is the bottom line to grading coins. Ultimately, it comes down to whether the buyer likes the coin and how much he or she is willing to pay for it.

1925-D MERCURY DIME

A LITTLE BACKGROUND

Since the early days of coin collecting, buying through the mail has been a convenient way for collectors to acquire coins. As a result, there has always been a need in numismatics for a concise way to classify the amount of wear on a coin and its condition in general.

In September 1888, Dr. George Heath, a physician in

Monroe, Michigan, published a four-page pamphlet titled *The American Numismatist.* Publication of subsequent issues led to the founding of the American Numismatic Association, and *The Numismatist*, as it's known today, is the association's official journal. Heath's first issues were largely devoted to selling world coins from his collection. There were no formal grades listed with the coins and their prices, but the following statement by Heath indicates that condition was a consideration for early collectors:

"The coins are in above average condition," Heath wrote, "and so confident am I that they will give satisfaction, that I agree to refund the money in any unsatisfactory sales on the return of the coins."

1815 CAPPED BUST QUARTER

As coin collecting became more popular, grading became more formal. "Poor," "fair," "good," "fine," and "uncirculated" became common terms for grading coins. But modifiers, such as "about good," "very good," "extremely fine," and "about uncirculated," were soon added to these basic terms to describe coins that fell in between the major classifications. The modified terms indicated a desire for more precision in grading coins but also reflected the process' subjective nature.

Books on coin grading started to appear in the late 1950s. They described and illustrated each coin grading term as they applied to each coin type. The books brought more universal definition to grading, though the process will forever maintain a certain degree of subjectivity.

The most common grading terminology used today is a combination of adjectives and numbers, as described below. The numbers range from 1 to 70, with mint-state, or uncirculated, grades beginning at 60.

GRADING CIRCULATED COINS

Following are commonly used terms and descriptions for grading circulated coins (those with wear on them) from best to worst. The complete term – adjective and number – is given first;

the commonly used shorthand version follows in parenthesis. Sometimes just the shorthand letters are used without the accompanying number.

Silver dollars are used to illustrate each term.

▶ ABOUT UNCIRCULATED-50 (AU-50)

Just a slight trace of wear, the result of brief exposure to circulation or light rubbing from mishandling, may be evident on the highest design areas. These imperfections may appear as scratches or dull spots, along with bag marks or edge nicks. At least half of the original mint luster generally is still evident.

▶ EXTREMELY FINE-40 (EF-40 OR XF-40)

Only slight evidence of wear is present on the design's highest points, particularly in hair lines on the obverse portrait. A trace of mint luster may still show in protected areas of the coin's surface.

▶ VERY FINE-20 (VF-20)

Light wear can be seen on the fine points in the design, though it may remain sharp overall. Although the details may be slightly smooth, all lettering and major features must remain sharp.

▶ FINE-12 (F-12)

Wear is moderate to considerable but generally even on all high points of the design. All elements of the design and lettering remain bold. On 20th-century and later coins, the rim must be fully raised and sharp.

MS-70
The grade mint state-70 (MS-70) describes a flawless coin. The standard provides a theoretical top to the circulation-strike grading scale.

► VERY GOOD-8 (VG-8)

The coin will show considerable wear, with most detail points worn nearly smooth. On 20th-century and later coins, the rim will start to merge with the lettering.

► GOOD-4 (G-4)

Only the basic design remains distinguishable in outline form. All detail points are worn smooth. The rims are almost merging with the lettering.

GRADING UNCIRCULATED COINS

The subjectivity of grading and the trend toward more classifications becomes more acute when venturing into uncirculated, or mint-state, coins. A small difference of one or two grade points can mean a difference in value of hundreds or even thousands of dollars. In addition, the standards are more difficult to articulate in writing and illustrate through drawings or photographs. Thus, the possibilities for differences of opinion on one or two grade points increase in uncirculated coins.

Back in Dr. George Heath's day and continuing through the 1960s, a coin was either uncirculated or it wasn't. Little distinction was made between uncirculated coins of varying condition, largely because there was little if any difference in value.

MS-65 SILVER DOLLAR

MS-63 SILVER DOLLAR

But as collectible coins increased in value and buyers of uncirculated coins became more picky, distinctions within uncirculated grades started to surface. By the 1970s, two terms were used to grade uncirculated coins: (1) mint state-60 (MS-60), which was a "typical uncirculated" coin, and (2) mint state-65 (MS-65), which was a "choice uncirculated" coin. By the 1980s, four grades of uncirculated – the two listed above plus MS-63 and MS-67 – were used for popular upper-end coins, such as silver dollars.

Then in 1986, a new entity appeared that has changed the nature of grading and trading uncirculated coins ever since. A group of dealers formed the Professional Coin Grading Service. For a fee, collectors can submit a coin through an authorized PCGS dealer and receive back a professional opinion of its grade.

After grading, the coin is encapsulated in an inert, hard-plastic holder with a serial number and the service's opinion on its grade indicated on the holder. The holders quickly earned the nickname "slabs."

In one of its most far-reaching moves, PCGS said it would use all 11 increments of uncirculated on the 70-point numerical scale: MS-60, MS-61, MS-62, MS-63, MS-64, MS-65, MS-66, MS-67, MS-68, MS-69, and MS-70.

Several other commercial grading services followed in the steps of PCGS, and third-party grading is now an accepted part of the hobby.

How should a collector approach the buying and grading of uncirculated coins? Collecting uncirculated coins worth thousands

WHY 1 TO 70?

1805 LARGE CENT

The 1-to-70 numerical grading scale is based on a system used by Dr. William H. Sheldon in his book *Early American Cents*, first published in 1949. He used the scale to designate the condition of U.S. large cents, struck from 1793 through 1857 before they were replaced by the smaller 1-cent coin used today.

"On this scale," Sheldon wrote, "1 means that the coin is identifiable and not mutilated – no more than that. A 70-coin is one in flawless Mint State, exactly as it left the dies, with perfect mint color and without a blemish or nick."

Sheldon's scale also had its pragmatic side. At the time, a No. 2 large cent was worth about twice a No. 1 coin. A No. 4 was worth about twice a No. 2, and so on up the scale.

1927 GOLD $20 IN PCGS HOLDER

of dollars implies a higher level of numismatic expertise by the buyer. Those buyers without that level of expertise should cut their teeth on less expensive coins, as outlined in this book, just as today's experienced collectors did.

GRADING PROOF COINS

Because proof coins are struck by a special process, they receive their own grading designation. A coin does not start out being a proof and then become mint state if it becomes worn. Once a proof coin, always a proof coin.

PROOF 1983 OLYMPIC SILVER DOLLAR

In grading proof coins, the term proof always precedes the numerical designation, such as proof-65, proof-55, and proof-45.

HOW TO LEARN MORE ABOUT GRADING

▶ BOOKS

The two most widely used grading books are *The Official American Numismatic Association Grading Standards for United States Coins* (Whitman Publishing), edited by Kenneth Bressett, and *Photograde* (Zyrus Press Publishing) by James F. Ruddy. Both books illustrate and describe each specific U.S. coin type in each grade.

ANA GRADING GUIDE

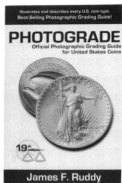

PHOTOGRADE

One or both books are widely available at coin shops and shows, larger bookstores, and on-line book sellers such as Numismaster (www.shopnumismaster.com).

▶ AMERICAN NUMISMATIC ASSOCIATION

The ANA (www.money.org) offers grading seminars at its two annual conventions, various other conventions hosted by state and regional organizations, and at its Summer Seminar series, held annually at the association's headquarters in Colorado Springs, Colorado. The ANA also offers correspondence courses on grading.

GRADING WORLD COINS

Because of the wide scope of world coins, there is no comprehensive grading guide for the field. But the general descriptions for circulated coins given here can be applied to world coins, too. Traditionally, just the adjectives are used in grading world coins ("good," "fine," "extremely fine," and so on), not the accompanying numbers.

▶ EXPERIENCE

Book knowledge and seminar knowledge can form an excellent basis for learning how to grade coins, but there's no substitute for simply looking at a lot of coins and learning to make judgments on condition and its relationship to value for yourself.

The searches of coin rolls described in various chapters in this book are a good starting point. As you examine each coin in a roll, check its condition with a magnifying glass. Do some look better than others? If so, why? What points in the coin's design tend to show wear?

For example, the search of five nickel rolls described in Chapter 4 turned up seven 1964 coins in varying conditions. Lining up some or all of the examples from worst to best is a good exercise in learning how to grade coins. Comparing them side by side illustrates how the Jefferson nickel looks as it begins to wear and which design areas tend to show the wear.

Shops and shows are also good places to look at lots of coins. Take your magnifying glass with you. If you see two coins of the same type and date but with different grades and prices, compare the two side by side and see what judgments you can make yourself about their condition.

Just like buying a used car, ultimately it comes down to whether a buyer likes the coin and is willing to pay the price.

PART 5

TAKING THE NEXT STEP

What to do when you're ready
to move up from the basics

CHAPTER 24

THE COIN COMMUNITY

Coin collecting can accommodate any personality type. For those who like solitude, there can be peaceful evenings searching rolls of coins, admiring a completed collection or one in progress, or opening a book or magazine on the subject. For those who like camaraderie, there is an entire community out there that shares their interest and numerous venues for bringing them together.

Following is an overview of the coin community at large and resources for learning more about coins.

ORGANIZATIONS

▶ NATIONAL

The American Numismatic Association (www.money.org), founded in 1891 and federally chartered, is the nation's largest organization for coin collectors. Its headquarters in Colorado Springs, Colorado, houses a first-class museum, the Edward C. Rochette Money Museum, which is open to the public.

ANA HEADQUARTERS

Membership benefits include a subscription to *The Numismatist*, the association's official journal. Each monthly issue features articles on a wide range of numismatic topics along with reports on association news and events.

Members can also borrow books, auction catalogs, slide sets, and videos from the ANA's library, the Dwight N. Manley Library, which boasts more than 50,000 items. Members who borrow items pay for postage and insurance but no additional fee.

ANA MUSEUM

The ANA sponsors seminars on a wide range of numismatic topics at various locales throughout the country. Prominent among them is the association's Summer Seminar series, held annually in late June and early July at its headquarters in Colorado Springs. Attendance at the multiday courses is designed to be affordable with a variety of lodging options and a meal plan.

The ANA also takes its seminar program on the road to the association's two annual conventions and to events sponsored by other numismatic organizations.

▶ REGIONAL

Regional coin organizations focus their activities on a certain part of the country, such as the Northeast or Midwest. Residency in the region, however, is usually not required for membership.

Prominent among these groups are the Central States Numismatic Society, Great Eastern Numismatic Association, New England Numismatic Association, and Pacific Northwest Numismatic Association. In addition, the Florida United Numismatists sponsors a large show and convention in January each year and boasts a large regional following in the Southeast.

See the Web site listings below for contact information for most of these organizations.

▶ STATE

Most states have clubs that focus on numismatic events and interests specific to the state. Again, residency in the state is usually not required for membership. See the Club Directory section of the ANA Web site listed below for information on state numismatic organizations.

▶ LOCAL

Many cities large and small have local coin clubs that meet regularly. The Club Directory section of the ANA Web site can help locate a club in or near a specific city. The events listings in local newspapers may help, too.

▶ SPECIAL INTEREST

Some clubs focus on a specific collecting interest, such as commemoratives, silver dollars, or coins of a particular country. They draw their membership nationally and keep in touch through a quarterly or monthly journal. They also meet at larger numismatic events, such as the ANA conventions.

See the Club Directory section of the ANA Web site for listings and contact information.

▶ SHOWS

Most numismatic organizations sponsor conventions and shows as part of their activities. They range from multiday events with a national or even world focus, such as the ANA's annual conventions, to smaller one-day events sponsored by the local coin club.

The events usually include a bourse, an area where dealers set-up to buy and sell coins. The local events may have a couple of dozen dealers; the larger events can have hundreds of dealers and booths for the U.S. Mint and other world mints. Both, however, give collectors the chance to look at a lot of coins in one location.

The larger events also feature educational opportunities, such as competitive exhibits and seminars.

Numismatic periodicals, such as the monthly *Coins* magazine, available on many newsstands, and the weekly *Numismatic News,* list upcoming shows throughout the country. The Numismaster Web site (see listings below) and the ANA Web site also list upcoming events.

BOOKS

The following books, all by Krause Publications, provide more information on coins and can also help new collectors take the next step in their collecting pursuits. They are available at most bookstores, online booksellers, or directly from the publisher at www.krausebooks.com.

▶ NORTH AMERICAN COINS AND PRICES

The bulk of this book is value listings for U.S., Canadian, and Mexican coins, but it also provides basic information on grading, how coins are made, assembling a collection, caring for coins, and market updates. New editions are published annually.

▶ STANDARD CATALOG OF WORLD COINS

This multivolume series, published since 1972 and known worldwide, lists and values every coin produced in the world since 1601. The books are broken down by century, and each volume can be purchased individually. Some volumes are available on compact discs. Downloads covering selected individual countries are also available.

▶ U.S. COINS & CURRENCY

Part of the Warman's Companion series, this book provides comprehensive coverage of U.S. coins and extensive coverage of U.S. paper money, including background information on each type of note. Introductory chapters cover some basic information about collecting U.S. coins and paper money.

▶ U.S. COIN DIGEST

This hardcover book with a spiral binding provides comprehensive listings and values for all U.S. coins. Introductory material covers some of the basics of coin collecting. New editions are published annually.

▶ WARMAN'S COINS & PAPER MONEY

Geared toward new collectors, this book is a value and identification guide for U.S., Canadian, Mexican, and other world coins and paper money. The large-format book is extensively illustrated.

▶ WORLD COINS & CURRENCY

Part of the Warman's Companion series, this book provides a good overview of world coinage and paper money. It's a lower-cost alternative to the much bigger *Standard Catalog of World Coins*.

PERIODICALS

The following publications provide news and information on a wide range of numismatic topics. In addition to their editorial content, their advertising provides a shop-at-home marketplace for coins from dealers nationwide.

▶ COINS

This monthly magazine (www.coinsmagazine.net) is available by subscription and on many newsstands. Its features and columns focus on U.S. coins but also cover the gamut of world numismatics. A U.S. coin value guide is included in each issue.

▶ NUMISMATIC NEWS

This weekly tabloid (www.numismaticnews.net), founded in 1952, focuses on U.S. hobby news and events but also includes features and columns covering a wide range of topics. A monthly value-guide supplement provides current listings for selected U.S. coins and market commentary and analysis. It's available by subscription and on some larger newsstands.

▶ WORLD COIN NEWS

Similar in format to *Numismatic News*, the monthly *World Coin News* (www.worldcoinnews.net) focuses on non-U.S. issues. It's available by subscription and on some larger newsstands.

WEB SITES

The following Web sites provide more information and resources on numismatic organizations, shows, publications, and coin collecting in general.

▶ WWW.CENTRALSTATES.INFO

Site for the Central States Numismatic Society. Provides news and information on this regional organization.

▶ WWW.CMM.GOB.MX

Site for the Casa de Moneda de México, Mexico's official mint.

▶ WWW.COINSMAGAZINE.NET

Site for *Coins* magazine. Includes subscription information and selected articles.

▶ WWW.FUNTOPICS.COM

Site for the Florida United Numismatists. Provides news and information on the organization.

▶ WWW.KRAUSEBOOKS.COM

Source for coin books published by Krause Publications.

▶ WWW.MINT.CA

Site for the Royal Canadian Mint, Canada's official mint. Includes ordering information for current issues.

▶ WWW.MONEY.ORG

Site for the American Numismatic Association, the nation's largest organization for coin collectors. Provides membership and collecting information, association news, a club directory, and information on upcoming events.

▶ WWW.NENACOIN.ORG

Site for the New England Numismatic Association. Provides news and information on this regional organization.

▶ WWW.NUMISMASTER.COM

Sponsored by the publisher of *Numismatic News*, *Coins* magazine, and its related publications, the Numismaster site provides news and features, a collection management system, value guides, and more. A subscription is required to access some parts of the site.

► WWW.NUMISMATICNEWS.NET

Site for the weekly *Numismatic News*. Includes subscription information and selected articles.

► WWW.PNNA.ORG

Site for the Pacific Northwest Numismatic Association. Provides news and information on this regional organization.

► WWW.ROYALMINT.COM

Site for The Royal Mint of Great Britain, the country's official mint. Includes ordering information for current issues.

► WWW.USMINT.GOV

Site for the U.S. Mint. Provides new-issue and historical information. Collectors can also order current Mint products, such as commemoratives, proof sets, and uncirculated sets.

► WWW.WORLDCOINNEWS.NET

Site for the monthly *World Coin News*. Includes subscription information and selected articles.

CHAPTER 25

MOVING UP

1916 STANDING LIBERTY QUARTER

F or some collectors, searching rolls of coins, watching their pocket change, buying new issues from the U.S. Mint, and buying inexpensive coins at shows or shops suit them just fine. They enjoy collecting at this level, are comfortable with it, and have no desire to move beyond it, nor should they feel any pressure to do so.

For others, however, searching rolls of Lincoln cents merely whets their appetite for something bigger. For them, more than 200 years of U.S. coinage and centuries more of world coinage lie waiting. Gold coins, silver dollars, classic designs, and legendary world coinage can all provide a collecting experience rich in history and pride in ownership.

1750 SHILLING OF GREAT BRITAIN

Unlike plucking coins from circulation at face value, however, moving up to coins like the ones mentioned above may require an outlay of hundreds or even thousands of dollars. That increases the chances for making mistakes, but the following tips for collecting more expensive coins will help limit those mistakes and lead to a rewarding collecting pastime.

1921 PEACE DOLLAR

COLLECT WHAT YOU LIKE

This remains coin-collecting rule No. 1 no matter the price. Collectors should always pursue a particular series or type set because something about it catches their interest. They shouldn't pursue it merely because others have said that's what they should collect or others have opined that it would be a good investment.

It may be the design. It may be the composition. It may be the subject depicted on the coin. It may be the country. In may be the era. Whatever the reason, the coins that capture an individual's interest are the coins he or she should collect.

STUDY

Once that coin series or type has captured your interest, learn as much about it as you can. The word "study" is often associated with drudgery, but that is not the case if you have an intrinsic interest in the subject (remember: collect what you like).

It starts by learning the history of the country that issued the coin and the era in which it was issued. U.S. coins, for example, changed compositions at various times in the country's history in response to economic and political considerations. Learning a coin's historical context leads to a greater appreciation and understanding of the issue.

Next, learn about the coin itself. Specialized books and magazine articles focus on a particular series, such as Lincoln cents, Franklin half dollars, or Morgan silver dollars. This literature recounts the coin's history – how it came to be, who designed it, background on the design itself, and why it was

discontinued if it is a
design or denomination
no longer produced.

These books and
articles can also provide
important information
on individual dates within
a series – which ones are
common, which ones are scarce, subtle design
changes from one year to the next, which
dates usually have strong strikes, and which
dates usually have weak strikes.

They may also provide information on
grading the series, but a grading book, such
as *The Official American Numismatic
Association Grading Standards for United
States Coins* or *Photograde*, or both, should
be a standard purchase for any coin collector, especially one
pursuing more expensive coins. The book should be kept handy,
referred to time and again, and eventually be worn out from use.

Finally, when you choose a type or series on which to focus,
take advantage of every opportunity to look at a lot of examples
of the coins at shows and shops. Take your magnifying glass with
you. Compare coins of the same date; compare different coins of
different dates. Compare condition and asking prices. Ultimately,
you are the final judge as to whether you like the coin and are
willing to pay the price.

1908-O BARBER HALF DOLLAR

1903-S BARBER DIME

MEET SOME DEALERS

Like shows, professional coin dealers can run the gamut from small-town, one-person operations to larger firms occupying multistory buildings in metropolitan areas. Which one is right for you?

Choosing a coin dealer to work with in building your collection is like choosing any enterprise with which you do business. You walk into the business and you're just comfortable there. Maybe it's because you were greeted with a friendly hello and smile when you walked in. Maybe it's because you were allowed to browse and weren't pressured into a sale. Maybe it's because the business owner or an employee was knowledgeable and took the time to explain things and answer questions.

Or maybe it's because a friend or relative recommended the business. Whatever the reason, you end up going back and you develop a relationship with the business. When you walk through the front door, the business owner or employees know you and know your history as a customer.

The same is true with coin dealers. Some may not hit it off with you, but one or more others may. Developing a business relationship with one or more dealers can be a great asset in building collection. The dealer knows what you want and your price range, and can look for coins you want when the dealer is on a buying trip.

ITS OK TO BARGAIN

It's OK to bargain with dealers at shows or shops, but be reasonable with your offers. It's OK to ask, "Is that your best price?"

It's not OK to berate a dealer if you think his or her prices are too high. Just move on to the next dealer at the show or move on to the next shop. The market ultimately will tell the dealer if his or her prices are too high.

1913-D BUFFALO NICKEL

1924 BUFFALO NICKEL

Oftentimes dealers will volunteer a small discount from the marked prices if you buy more than one coin. For example, if you select two coins and the total of the marked prices comes to $107, the dealer might take just $100. Repeat business with the dealer might yield some discounts, too.

AUCTIONS

Coin auctions are another fun and exciting way to build a collection. Some of numismatics' great rarities have made national headlines when they were sold at auction.

Major coin auctions are often staged as stand-alone events in ballrooms of large hotels. Many of the larger coin shows, including the annual ANA conventions, have auctions as part of the event's activities.

COIN AUCTION

Auction companies usually require that you register as a bidder before the sale, but you don't have to be present to bid. Bids can also be submitted by phone and on-line.

Auctions are great educational opportunities even if you never bid at one. The major auction companies produce high-quality catalogs illustrating and describing each lot in the sale. The descriptions can be quite lengthy and filled with a wealth of historical and collecting information. The catalogs can be purchased in advance of the sale and are great additions to a numismatic library.

Watching an auction in person is also a great experience. By simply observing, a new collector can get a feel for how auctions work and their pace. And after the sale, the prices-realized list provides important market information.

If you do intend to bid at an auction, be sure to read carefully the sale terms as printed in the catalog. A thorough understanding of the auction company's obligations and your obligations as a bidder can prevent surprises and misunderstandings. For example, most auction companies charge a buyer's premium of 10 percent to 15 percent, so a collector must take this surcharge into consideration when determining how much to bid on a coin.

COINS AS INVESTMENTS

Coins should not be purchased solely as investments unless you are playing the highest end of the market and buying some of the field's greatest rarities. That's not to say, however, that coins can't be good investments.

Some fabulous coin collections have been sold over the years and have reaped large sums for their owners or heirs. The biographies of those who assembled these great collections have one thing in common: These people were collectors first. They assembled these collections because they loved collecting coins. They studied the subject and were well schooled on what they were

1911-D GOLD
$2.50

buying. They truly enjoyed their collections, and in time, they reaped financial rewards from them, too.

Be a collector first. Study what you're collecting. Know your coins. Make wise purchases. If you do, the financial aspects of coin collecting will take care of themselves.

Coins can increase in value over time; they can also decrease. But if you're a collector first, the market can never take away the enjoyment you get from the hobby.

1873-CC GOLD $10

CHAPTER 26

U.S. COINS ON REVIEW

U.S. coins provide a wealth of material for collectors. They offer a wide range of compositions, design styles and subjects, and sizes. The following pages provide a summary of all U.S. coins struck for circulation. For a complete listing of U.S. coins, including individual date and mintmark combinations and values in various grades, see the book *U.S. Coin Digest*.

Value ranges listed below are approximate retail prices (what you can expect to pay if you purchase the coin from a dealer) for more common dates in the series grading F-12 to XF-40. Key dates have higher values.

Diameters are in millimeters. Weights are in grams. Actual silver and gold weights are in troy ounces.

The various coin types are listed by their names commonly used in the hobby. The name usually refers to the main obverse design, but some coins are known by their designers' names.

HALF CENT

LIBERTY CAP, HEAD FACING LEFT

Dates: 1793. Designer: Henry Voigt. Diameter: 22. Weight: 6.74. Composition: 100-percent copper. Value: $8,500-$27,000.

LIBERTY CAP, HEAD FACING RIGHT

Dates: 1794-1797. Designer: Robert Scot (1794) and John Smith Gardner (1795). Diameter: 23.5. Weight: 6.74 (1794-1795) and 5.44 (1795-1797). Composition: 100-percent copper. Value: $750-$6,000.

DRAPED BUST

Dates: 1800, 1802-1808. Designer: Robert Scot. Diameter: 23.5. Weight: 5.44. Composition: 100-percent copper. Value: $85-$550.

CLASSIC HEAD

Dates: 1809-1811, 1825-1826, 1828-1829, 1831-1836. Designer: John Reich. Diameter: 23.5. Weight: 5.44. Composition: 100-percent copper. Value: $75-$550.

BRAIDED HAIR

Dates: 1840-1857. Designer: Christian Gobrecht. Diameter: 23. Weight: 5.44. Composition: 100-percent copper. Value: $80-$3,000.

LARGE CENT

FLOWING HAIR, CHAIN REVERSE

Dates: 1793. Designer: Henry Voigt. Diameter: 26-27. Weight: 13.48.
Composition: 100-percent copper. Value: $17,750-$63,500.

FLOWING HAIR, WREATH REVERSE

Dates: 1793. Designer: Henry Voigt. Diameter: 26-28. Weight: 13.48.
Composition: 100-percent copper. Value: $4,750-$14,000.

LIBERTY CAP

Dates: 1793-1796. Designer: Joseph Wright (1793-1795) and John Smith
Gardner (1795-1796). Diameter: 29. Weight: 13.48 (1793-1795) and 10.89
(1795-1796). Composition: 100-percent copper. Value: $675-$4,750.

DRAPED BUST

Dates: 1796-1807. Designer: Robert Scot. Diameter: 29. Weight: 10.98.
Composition: 100-percent copper. Value: $150-$5,500.

CLASSIC HEAD

Dates: 1808-1814. Designer: John Reich. Diameter: 29. Weight: 10.98.
Composition: 100-percent copper. Value: $200-$1,500.

CORONET

Dates: 1816-1839. Designer: Robert Scot. Diameter: 28-29. Weight: 10.89.
Composition: 100-percent copper. Value: $30-$200.

BRAIDED HAIR

Dates: 1839-1857. Designer: Christian Gobrecht. Diameter: 27.5. Weight:
10.89. Composition: 100-percent copper. Value: $25-$100.

SMALL CENT

FLYING EAGLE

Dates: 1856-1858. Designer: James B. Longacre. Diameter: 19. Weight: 4.67. Composition: 88-percent copper, 12-percent nickel. Value: $40-$150.

INDIAN HEAD

Dates: 1859-1909. Designer: James B. Longacre. Diameter: 19. Weight: 4.67 (1859-1864) and 3.11 (1864-1909). Composition: 88 percent copper, 12-percent nickel (1859-1864) and 95-percent copper, 5-percent tin and zinc (1864-1909). Value: $2.50-$275.

LINCOLN, WHEAT REVERSE

Dates: 1909-1958. Designer: Victor D. Brenner. Diameter: 19. Weight: 3.11 (1909-1942, 1944-1958) and 2.7 (1943). Composition: 95-percent copper, 5-percent tin and zinc (1909-1942); zinc-coated steel (1943); and 95-percent copper, 5-percent zinc (1944-1958). Value: 25 cents-$100.

LINCOLN, MEMORIAL REVERSE

Dates: 1959-2008. Reverse designer: Frank Gasparro. Diameter: 19. Weight: 3.11 (1959-1982) and 2.5 (1982-2008). Composition: 95-percent copper, 5-percent tin and zinc (1959-1962); 95-percent copper, 5 percent zinc (1962-1982); and 97.6-percent zinc, 2.4-percent copper (1982-2008). Value: Nominal in circulated grades except for some scarce varieties.

LINCOLN, LINCOLN BICENTENNIAL REVERSES

Dates: 2009. See chapter 3.

LINCOLN, UNION SHIELD REVERSE

Dates: 2010-present. Reverse designers: Lyndall Bass and Joseph Menna. Diameter: 19. Weight: 2.5. Composition: 97.6-percent zinc, 2.4-percent copper. Value: Nominal in circulated grades.

2-CENT

Dates: 1864-1873. Designer: James B. Longacre. Diameter: 23. Weight: 6.22. Composition: 95-percent copper, 5-percent tin and zinc. Value: $20-$150.

SILVER 3-CENT

TYPE 1 (NO OUTLINES IN STAR)

Dates: 1851-1853. Designer: James B. Longacre. Diameter: 14. Weight: 0.8. Composition: 75-percent silver, 25-percent copper. Actual silver weight: 0.0193. Value: $50-$70.

TYPE 2 (THREE OUTLINES IN STAR)

Dates: 1854-1858. Designer: James B. Longacre. Diameter: 14. Weight: 0.75. Composition: 90-percent silver, 10-percent copper. Actual silver weight: 0.0218. Value: $50-$120.

TYPE 3 (TWO OUTLINES IN STAR)

Dates: 1859-1873. Designer: James B. Longacre. Diameter: 14. Weight: 0.75. Composition: 90-percent silver, 10-percent copper. Actual silver weight: 0.0218. Value: $50-$700.

NICKEL 3-CENT

Dates: 1865-1889. Designer: James B. Longacre. Diameter: 17.9. Weight: 1.94. Composition: 75-percent copper, 25-percent nickel. Value: $20-$450.

HALF DIME

FLOWING HAIR

Dates: 1794-1795. Designer: Robert Scot.
Diameter: 16.5. Weight: 1.35. Composition:
89.24-percent silver, 10.76-percent
copper. Actual silver weight: 0.0388. Value:
$1,875-$7,325.

DRAPED BUST, SMALL EAGLE

Dates: 1796-1797. Designer: Robert Scot.
Diameter: 16.5. Weight: 1.35. Composition:
89.24-percent silver, 10.76-percent
copper. Actual silver weight: 0.0388. Value:
$3,000-$9,800.

DRAPED BUST, HERALDIC EAGLE

Dates: 1800-1803, 1805. Designer:
Robert Scot. Diameter: 16.5. Weight:
1.35. Composition: 89.24-percent silver,
10.76-percent copper. Actual silver weight:
0.0388. Value: $1,875-$7,000.

LIBERTY CAP

Dates: 1829-1837. Designer: William
Kneass. Diameter: 15.5. Weight: 1.35.
Composition: 89.24-percent silver,
10.76-percent copper. Actual silver weight:
0.0388. Value: $60-$185.

SEATED LIBERTY

Dates: 1837-1873. Designer: Christian
Gobrecht. Diameter: 15.5. Weight: 1.34
(1837-1853) and 1.24 (1853-1873).
Composition: 90-percent silver, 10-percent
copper. Actual silver weight: 0.388 (1837-
1853) and 0.0362 (1853-1873). Value:
$25-$250.

NICKEL 5-CENT

SHIELD

Dates: 1866-1883. Designer: James B. Longacre. Diameter: 20.5. Weight: 5. Composition: 75-percent copper, 25-percent nickel. Value: $30-$200.

LIBERTY

Dates: 1883-1913. Designer: Charles E. Barber. Diameter: 21.2. Weight: 5. Composition: 75-percent copper, 25-percent nickel. Value: $4-$100.

BUFFALO

Dates: 1913-1921, 1923-1931. 1934-1938. Designer: James Earle Fraser. Diameter: 21.2. Weight: 5. Composition: 75-percent copper, 25-percent nickel. Value: $2-$250.

JEFFERSON

Dates: 1938-2003. Designer: Felix Schlag. Diameter: 21.2. Weight: 5. Composition: 75-percent copper, 25-percent nickel (1938-1942, 1946-2003); 56-percent copper, 35-percent silver, 9-percent manganese (1942-1945). Actual silver weight: 0.0563 (1942-1945). Values: 25 cents-$3 for pre-1959 dates.

JEFFERSON, WESTWARD JOURNEY SERIES

Dates: 2004-2005. See chapter 4.

JEFFERSON, NEW PORTRAIT, ENHANCED REVERSE

Dates: 2006-present. Obverse designers: Jamie N. Franki and Donna Weaver. Reverse designers: Felix Schlag and John Mercanti. Diameter: 21.2. Weight: 5. Composition: 75-percent copper, 25-percent nickel. Values: Nominal in circulated grades.

DIME

DRAPED BUST, SMALL EAGLE

Dates: 1796-1797. Designer: Robert Scot. Diameter: 19. Weight: 2.7. Composition: 89.24-percent silver, 10.76-percent copper. Actual silver weight: 0.0775. Values: $5,350-$13,150.

DRAPED BUST, HERALDIC EAGLE

Dates: 1798, 1800-1805, 1807. Designer: Robert Scot. Diameter: 19. Weight: 2.7. Composition: 89.24-percent silver, 10.76-percent copper. Actual silver weight: 0.0775. Values: $1,200-$2,750.

LIBERTY CAP

Dates: 1809, 1811, 1814, 1820-1825, 1827-1837. Designer: John Reich. Diameter: 18.8 (1809-1828) and 18.5 (1828-1837). Weight: 2.7. Composition: 89.24-percent silver, 10.76-percent copper. Actual silver weight: 0.0775. Values: $50-$450.

SEATED LIBERTY

Dates: 1837-1891. Designer: Christian Gobrecht. Diameter: 17.9. Weight: 2.67 (1837-1853), 2.49 (1853-1873), and 2.5 (1873-1891). Composition: 90-percent silver, 10-percent copper. Actual silver weight: 0.0773 (1837-1853), 0.072 (1853-1873), and 0.0723 (1873-1891). Values: $10-$1,000.

BARBER

Dates: 1892-1916. Designer: Charles E. Barber. Diameter: 17.9. Weight: 2.5. Composition: 90-percent silver, 10-percent copper. Actual silver weight: 0.0724. Values: $4-$500.

MERCURY

Dates: 1916-1921, 1923-1931, 1934-1945. Designer: Adolph A. Weinman. Diameter: 17.9. Weight: 2.5. Composition: 90-percent silver, 10-percent copper. Actual silver weight: 0.0724. Values: $3-$50.

ROOSEVELT

Dates: 1946-present. Designer: John R. Sinnock. Diameter: 17.9. Weight: 2.5 (1946-1964) and 2.27 (1965-present). Composition: 90-percent silver, 10-percent copper (1946-1964) and clad layers of 75-percent copper and 25-percent nickel bonded to a pure-copper core (1965-present). Actual silver weight: 0.0724 (1946-1964). Values: up to $4 for some pre-1965 dates.

20-CENT

Dates: 1875-1878. Designer: William Barber. Diameter: 22. Weight: 5. Composition: 90-percent silver, 10-percent copper. Actual silver weight: 0.1447. Values: $120-$400.

QUARTER

DRAPED BUST, SMALL EAGLE

Dates: 1796. Designer: Robert Scot. Diameter: 27.5. Weight: 6.74.
Composition: 89.24-percent silver, 10.76-percent copper. Actual silver
weight: 0.1935. Values: $30,000-$42,500.

DRAPED BUST, HERALDIC EAGLE

Dates: 1804-1807. Designer: Robert Scot. Diameter: 27.5. Weight: 6.74.
Composition: 89.24-percent silver, 10.76-percent copper. Actual silver
weight: 0.1935. Values: $500-$2,850.

LIBERTY CAP

Dates: 1815, 1818-1825, 1827-1828, 1831-1838. Designer: John Reich
(1815-1828) and William Kneass (1831-1838). Diameter: 27 (1815-1828)
and 24.3 (1831-1838). Weight: 6.74. Composition: 89.24-percent silver,
10.76-percent copper. Actual silver weight: 0.1935. Values: $100-$1,500.

SEATED LIBERTY

Dates: 1838-1891. Designer: Christian Gobrecht. Diameter: 24.3.
Weight: 6.68 (1838-1853), 6.22 (1853-1873), and 6.25 (1873-1891).
Composition: 90-percent silver, 10-percent copper. Actual silver weight:
0.1934 (1838-1853) and 0.18 (1853-1891). Values: $30-$1,200.

BARBER

Dates: 1892-1916. Designer: Charles E. Barber. Diameter: 24.3. Weight:
6.25. Composition: 90-percent silver, 10-percent copper. Actual silver
weight: 0.18. Values: $20-$400.

STANDING LIBERTY

Dates: 1916-1921, 1923-1930. Designer: Hermon A. MacNeil. Diameter:
24.3. Weight: 6.25. Composition: 90-percent silver, 10-percent copper.
Actual silver weight: 0.18. Values: $10-$565.

WASHINGTON

Dates: 1932, 1934-1998. Designer: John Flanagan. Diameter: 24.3. Weight: 6.25 (1932-1964) and 5.67 (1965-1998). Composition: 90-percent silver, 10-percent copper (1932-1964) and clad layers of 75-percent copper and 25-percent nickel bonded to a pure-copper core (1965-1998). Actual silver weight: 0.18 (1946-1964). Values: $7-$75 for pre-1965 dates.

WASHINGTON, 50 STATE REVERSES

Dates: 1999-2008. See Chapter 6.

WASHINGTON, DISTRICT OF COLUMBIA AND U.S. TERRITORIES REVERSES

Dates: 2009. See Chapter 6.

WASHINGTON, AMERICA THE BEAUTIFUL REVERSES

Dates: 2010-2021. See Chapter 6.

HALF DOLLAR

FLOWING HAIR

Dates: 1794-1795. Designer: Robert Scot. Diameter: 32.5. Weight: 13.48.
Composition: 89.24-percent silver, 10.76-percent copper. Actual silver
weight: 0.3869. Value: $2,850-$17,500.

DRAPED BUST, SMALL EAGLE

Dates: 1796-1797. Designer: Robert Scot. Diameter: 32.5. Weight: 13.48.
Composition: 89.24-percent silver, 10.76-percent copper. Actual silver
weight: 0.3869. Value: $62,000-$128,000.

DRAPED BUST, HERALDIC EAGLE

Dates: 1801-1803, 1805-1807. Designer: Robert Scot. Diameter: 32.5.
Weight: 13.48. Composition: 89.24-percent silver, 10.76-percent copper.
Actual silver weight: 0.3869. Value: $300-$2,500.

LIBERTY CAP

Dates: 1807-1815, 1817-1836. Designer: John Reich (1807-1836).
Diameter: 32.5. Weight: 13.48. Composition: 89.24-percent silver,
10.76-percent copper. Actual silver weight: 0.3869. Value: $75-$750.

BUST

Dates: 1836-1839. Designer: Christian Gobrecht. Diameter: 30. Weight:
13.36. Composition: 90-percent silver, 10-percent copper. Actual silver
weight: 0.3867. Value: $80-$250.

SEATED LIBERTY

Dates: 1839-1891. Designer: Christian Gobrecht. Diameter: 30.6. Weight:
13.36 (1839-1853), 12.44 (1853-1873), and 12.5 (1873-1891).
Composition: 90-percent silver, 10-percent copper. Actual silver weight:
0.3867 (1839-1853), 0.36 (1853-1873), and 0.3618 (1873-1891). Value:
$50-$500.

BARBER

Dates: 1892-1915. Designer: Charles E. Barber. Diameter: 30.6. Weight: 12.5. Composition: 90-percent silver, 10-percent copper. Actual silver weight: 0.3618. Value: $30-$600.

WALKING LIBERTY

Dates: 1916-1921, 1923, 1927-1929, 1933-1947. Designer: Adolph A. Weinman. Diameter: 30.6. Weight: 12.5. Composition: 90-percent silver, 10-percent copper. Actual silver weight: 0.3618. Value: $15-$600.

FRANKLIN

Dates: 1948-1963. Designer: John R. Sinnock. Diameter: 30.6. Weight: 12.5. Composition: 90-percent silver, 10-percent copper. Actual silver weight: 0.3618. Value: Up to $25 for some dates in grade XF-40.

KENNEDY

Dates: 1964-present. Obverse designer: Gilroy Roberts. Reverse designer: Frank Gasparro. Diameter: 30.6. Weight: 12.5 (1964), 11.5 (1965-1970), and 11.34 (1971-present). Composition: 90-percent silver, 10-percent copper (1964); clad layers of 80-percent silver and 20-percent copper bonded to a core of 20.9-percent silver and 79.1-percent copper (1965-1970); and clad layers of 75-percent copper and 25-percent nickel bonded to a pure-copper core (1971-present). Actual silver weight: 0.3618 (1964) and 0.148 (1965-1970). Value: Up to $13 for 1964-dated coins in grade XF-40. Bullion value for coins dated 1965 through 1970. Nominal for all other dates in circulated grades.

SILVER DOLLAR

FLOWING HAIR

Dates: 1794-1795. Designer: Robert Scot. Diameter: 39-40. Weight: 26.96. Composition: 89.24-percent silver, 10.76-percent copper. Actual silver weight: 0.7737. Value: $7,250-$16,000.

DRAPED BUST, SMALL EAGLE

Dates: 1795-1798. Designer: Robert Scot. Diameter: 39-40. Weight: 26.96. Composition: 89.24-percent silver, 10.76-percent copper. Actual silver weight: 0.7737. Value: $4,000-$13,000.

DRAPED BUST, HERALDIC EAGLE

Dates: 1798-1804. Designer: Robert Scot. Diameter: 39-40. Weight: 26.96. Composition: 89.24-percent silver, 10.76-percent copper. Actual silver weight: 0.7737. Value: $1,750-$5,500.

SEATED LIBERTY

Dates: 1840-1873. Designer: Christian Gobrecht. Diameter: 38.1. Weight: 26.73. Composition: 90-percent silver, 10-percent copper. Actual silver weight: 0.7736. Value: $300-$1,500.

MORGAN

Dates: 1878-1904, 1921. Designer: George T. Morgan. Diameter: 38.1. Weight: 26.73. Composition: 90-percent silver, 10-percent copper. Actual silver weight: 0.7736. Value: $35-$1,000.

PEACE

Dates: 1921-1928, 1934-1935. Designer: Anthony de Francisci. Diameter: 38.1. Weight: 26.73. Composition: 90-percent silver, 10-percent copper. Actual silver weight: 0.7736. Value: $30-$40.

CLAD DOLLAR

EISENHOWER

Dates: 1971-1974, 1976, 1977-1978. Designer: Frank Gasparro. Diameter: 38.1. Weight: 22.68. Composition: 75-percent copper and 25-percent nickel bonded to a pure copper core. Value: Nominal in circulated grades.

ANTHONY

Dates: 1979-1981, 1999. Designer: Frank Gasparro. Diameter: 26.5. Weight: 8.1. Composition: clad layers of 75-percent copper and 25-percent nickel bonded to a pure copper core. Value: Nominal in circulated grades.

SACAGAWEA

Dates: 2000-2008. Obverse designer: Glenna Goodacre. Reverse designer: Thomas D. Rogers Sr. Diameter: 26.4 millimeters. Weight: 8.07 grams. Composition: 88.5-percent copper, 6-percent zinc, 3.5-percent manganese, 2-percent nickel. Value: Nominal in circulated grades.

SACAGAWEA, NATIVE AMERICAN REVERSES

Dates: 2009-present. See chapter 10.

PRESIDENTIAL

Dates: 2007-2016. See chapter 11.

GOLD DOLLAR

TYPE 1

Dates: 1849-1854. Designer: James B. Longacre. Diameter: 13. Weight: 1.672. Composition: 90-percent gold, 10-percent copper. Actual gold weight: 0.0484. Value: $150-$300.

TYPE 2

Dates: 1854-1856. Designer: James B. Longacre. Diameter: 15. Weight: 1.672. Composition: 90-percent gold, 10-percent copper. Actual gold weight: 0.0484. Value: $250-$600.

TYPE 3

Dates: 1856-1889. Designer: James B. Longacre. Diameter: 15. Weight: 1.672. Composition: 90-percent gold, 10-percent copper. Actual gold weight: 0.0484. Value: $200-$600.

GOLD $2.50

LIBERTY CAP

Dates: 1796-1798, 1802, 1804-1807.
Designer: Robert Scot. Diameter:
20. Weight: 4.37. Composition:
91.67-percent gold, 8.33-percent
copper. Actual gold weight: 0.1289.
Value: $4,250-$20,000.

TURBAN HEAD

Dates: 1808, 1821, 1824-1827,
1829-1834. Designer: John Reich.
Diameter: 20 (1808), 18.5 (1821-
1827), and 18.2 (1829-1834). Weight:
4.37. Composition: 91.67-percent
gold, 8.33-percent copper. Actual
gold weight: 0.1289. Value: $5,500-
$11,000.

CLASSIC HEAD

Date: 1834-1839. Designer: William
Kneass. Diameter: 18.2. Weight: 4.18.
Composition: 89.92-percent gold,
10.8-percent copper. Actual gold
weight: 0.1209. Value: $500-$1,000.

CORONET HEAD

Dates: 1840-1907. Designer: Christian
Gobrecht. Diameter: 18. Weight:
4.18. Composition: 90-percent gold,
10-percent copper. Actual gold weight:
0.121. Value: $150-$500.

INDIAN HEAD

Dates: 1908-1915, 1925-1929.
Designer: Bela Lyon Pratt. Diameter:
18. Weight: 4.18. Composition:
90-percent gold, 10-percent copper.
Actual gold weight: 0.121. Value:
$200-$300.

GOLD $3

Dates: 1854-1889. Designer: James B. Longacre. Diameter: 20.5. Weight: 5.015. Composition: 90-percent gold, 10-percent copper. Actual gold weight: 0.1452. Value: $800-$2,000.

GOLD $5

LIBERTY CAP, SMALL EAGLE

Dates: 1795-1798. Designer: Robert Scot. Diameter: 25. Weight: 8.75. Composition: 91.67-percent gold, 8.33-percent copper. Actual gold weight: 0.258. Value: $20,000-$40,000.

LIBERTY CAP, HERALDIC EAGLE

Dates: 1795, 1797-1800, 1802-1807. Designer: Robert Scot. Diameter: 25. Weight: 8.75. Composition: 91.67-percent gold, 8.33-percent copper. Actual gold weight: 0.258. Value: $3,850-$7,500.

TURBAN HEAD

Dates: 1807-1815, 1818-1834. Designer: John Reich. Diameter: 25. Weight: 8.75. Composition: 91.67-percent, 8.33-percent copper. Actual gold weight: 0.258. Value: $3,000-$15,000.

CLASSIC HEAD

Dates: 1834-1838. Designer: William Kneass. Diameter: 22.5. Weight: 8.36. Composition: 89.92-percent gold, 10.08-percent copper. Actual gold weight: 0.2418. Value: $500-$900.

CORONET HEAD

Dates: 1839-1908. Designer: Christian Gobrecht. Diameter: 21.6. Weight: 8.359. Composition: 90-percent gold, 10-percent copper. Actual gold weight: 0.242. Value: $500-$2,500.

INDIAN HEAD

Dates: 1908-1916, 1929. Designer: Bela Lyon Pratt. Diameter: 21.6. Weight: 8.359. Composition: 90-percent gold, 10-percent copper. Actual gold weight: 0.242. Value: $500-$600.

GOLD $10

LIBERTY CAP, SMALL EAGLE

Dates: 1795-1797. Designer: Robert
Scot. Diameter: 33. Weight: 17.5.
Composition: 91.67-percent gold,
8.33-percent copper. Actual gold
weight: 0.5159. Value: $27,500-
$55,000.

LIBERTY CAP, HERALDIC EAGLE

Dates: 1797-1801, 1803-1804.
Designer: Robert Scot. Diameter:
33. Weight: 17.5. Composition:
91.67-percent gold, 8.33-percent
copper. Actual gold weight: 0.5159.
Value: $9,000-$20,000.

CORONET HEAD

Dates: 1838-1907. Designer: Christian
Gobrecht. Diameter: 27. Weight:
16.718. Composition: 90-percent gold,
10-percent copper. Actual gold weight:
0.4839. Value: $700-$2,000.

INDIAN HEAD

Dates: 1907-1916, 1920, 1926,
1930, 1932-1933. Designer: Augustus
Saint-Gaudens. Diameter: 27. Weight:
16.718. Composition: 90-percent gold,
10-percent copper. Actual gold weight:
0.4839. Value: $900-$1,000.

GOLD $20

LIBERTY

Dates: 1849-1907. Designer: James B. Longacre. Diameter: 34. Weight: 33.436. Composition: 90-percent gold, 10-percent copper. Actual gold weight: 0.9677. Value: $1,700-$2,500.

SAINT-GAUDENS

Dates: 1907-1916, 1920-1933. Designer: Augustus Saint-Gaudens. Diameter: 34. Weight: 33.436. Composition: 90-percent gold, 10-percent copper. Actual gold weight: 0.9677. Value: $1,700-$1,850.

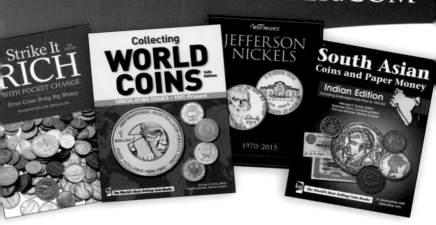